Because of

The Sacred Alchemy of a Mother's Unending Bond with Her Son in Spirit

RAINA IRENE

"What we know about 'Death' is the same thing we know about 'Life' –
*it is '**Love**' that bonds us together."*

–Raina Irene

Contents

Foreword

*O*nce in a blue moon you meet someone who touches something in your soul with their presence; they hold a gentle power you cannot help but feel drawn to. Then you hear their story, and it brings you to your knees. Raina is one of the most magical and powerful women I have ever met, and her journey of loss and love is unlike any other I have encountered. Her writing captures the essence of pain and possibility, the human pilgrimage with the divine etched into each word and sentiment. I wish I had the chance to meet Raina's son, and through her life-changing book, *Because of Josiah...* my heart knows I have.

This book is more than a journey, it's a tool for healing, and to support us through loss, love, and remembrance. It takes hope and transforms it from an idea to a completely tangible experience. As I read Raina's words, my heart broke a million times, yet I would not change anything because every word of Raina and Josiah mended my soul in places I didn't even know was broken.

This book will change lives and heal the deepest of wounds with the glimmer of light cast in each chapter. Thank you, Raina.

~Melissa Kim Corter
Author/ Speaker/ Intuitive Coach

Introduction

"Healing occurs when the light from above fills our being, transforming the light within, allowing us to shine a brighter light into the world."

~Josiah David

The Heart of the Mother

Sacred Mommaz,

I thank you, with everything I am, for being here with me.

On October 22, 2017, my heart stopped with *His*. My youngest child, my twenty-nine-year-old son, my baby Josiah, left planet Earth, changing the direction of all that I am, and all I would be. I know you know this identical state of existence. *That you're a bystander to the unreal.*

Grief has a way of cutting through you like no other emotion, shapeshifting the current of your DNA. The blood that once traveled your veins is replaced with tears, bypassing your shattered heart that cannot contain them. There is no way past this part. None! How my body can produce so much fluid repeatedly is illogical. Yet I never seem to dry out. Moments turn into days, then weeks, then months. And now I face years. In my process I have come to embrace my tears. I feel that when I cry, Josiah is close. So close that it overwhelms my heart to tears. The deeper I cry, the tighter his hug.

Even now, as I write to you, Grief engulfs me. She has become a part of me. She challenges my puzzled heart as it pounds. She begins to reproach me asking, "Who are you to share your story? Who are you to write a book? What words do you have to say?"

I catch the scorn and ridicule in her tone and reply, "A Mother! I am a mother whose son left way too early. A Mother in deep anguish, longing for the voice of her son." Every moment of every day I still pause, anticipating the phone to ring. His voice on the other end, speaking the dialect only I understand. *'Mom, I need you. Mom, what about this? Mom what about that? Mom guess what happened today! Who I met! What I did and what we talked about!'* and the, *'Guess what I want to do! What I want to create, and what I've discovered, that you need to know!'* I long for, *'I Love you,'* and the *'I love you, mores!'* I am a mother wanting to hear his triumphs and help him in every way she can. I'm a Mother!"

With tears flooding down my face and fear in my throat, I reach out, snatching back the puzzle piece that grief was attempting to steal, telling my challenged heart, "It's mine! Not one piece of this puzzle will leave the other!"

I am a Mother. My heart aches every day. And what I want to share is that this Mother has had profound experiences with her son in spirit. I want you, Sacred Mommaz, to know that your child is with you. Even in our deepest grief. Even when our tears flood from the abyss of our soul. Even when we question and search, "Where are they? Where are they?" I am a Mother that knows he is here. He shows up for me every day – in the tears, through the tears, and with the tears. He comes through.

Is it easy? NO! Nothing about this alteration of my life has been easy! There are days I want to check out and do nothing but watch Netflix and pretend. Oh, how I wish I could just pretend.

Then there are the glorious ways he shows up, like today. As I completed writing the above puzzle dialogue between my mind and my soul, this happened.

First let me say that I have had several experiences with Josiah, which I will share with you throughout this book. Just in the past week or so, I have had several dreams.

The first one: *Josiah was at my parents' home, my childhood home. He was sitting at the kitchen table; I was by the sink. We were just looking at each other. Then I woke. I was aware that there was nothing on the table or the kitchen counter, which was not the norm in my mother's kitchen. I felt like he was waiting for me.*

A few days later: *In the next dream, we were in what appeared to be my home. In my bedroom. He was in burgundy shorts, pacing impatiently. He was telling me that his shorts were too tight. He repeated that several times. I offered to get him another pair or go shopping. Then the scene changed. I was in an elevator with other mothers. I was saying "We are going to see the babies, right? We are going to see the babies?" Then the elevator went to the right on its side, down a corridor, like in a scene from Charlie and The Chocolate Factory. It came to a stop and I busted out a window of the elevator and jumped out.* (He was obviously getting impatient with me and we were outgrowing our present state, and I was determined to go see those babies. Our babies.)

A few more days went by. It was midnight when my memory kicked in. I sat straight up in bed, thinking, *I have his burgundy shorts*!!! They were neatly tucked away in a drawer. I laid there rustling through the meanings of both dreams. Josiah had been patiently waiting for me in the warm nurturing energy of my mother's kitchen. I was procrastinating, and he was getting impatient with me, wanting me to continue. I had to wait until morning, or I would have woken my husband, Richard. But let me tell you, as soon as I woke, I immediately found the shorts and searched the pockets for a hopeful clue that I may have missed the year prior. Nothing but a faint smell of him I inhaled. I brought them to my Healing Work room, hopeful they would be my muse.

Let me pause here to tell you about this space. I have spent most of my adult life learning and teaching about Holistic Health in some form or another. I am a Heart, Soul, Spirit Practitioner (you will learn how I received that title later in this book), but the best way to describe myself is "eclectic." I am a licensed Esthetician, a Reiki Master, and I have multiple certificates in Holistic Health; Spiritual Work; Emotional Healing; and Plant Medicine. Josiah referred to me as "My mom, The Oracle!", which of course I loved. My healing work room is where I go to do my sessions, write, or find solace. So "Workroom" or "Healing Room" are used interchangeably in these chapters.

Now, I folded his burgundy shorts neatly on the massage table next to my laptop, trusting they would speak to me. The very next day my friend Rachel came over. She is exceptional at *Psychometry* (the ability to discover facts about an event or person by touching objects associated with them.) I told her about the dreams in detail as we sat with Josiah's burgundy shorts between us. She began rubbing the shorts between her fingers.

"I can see him," she said, her eyes welling. "He is walking near a river. He has a staff in his hand, and he is looking for something." Then she released the shorts as we both began to cry.

"What is he looking for, Rachel?"

"I don't know, I don't know!" she murmured, mystified by what had just happened. Our tears were interrupted by the clock as it reminded Rachel it was time for her to leave for work.

Earlier that day I had felt the need to take one of my stones to my Healing Room. Nothing unusual about that. It is common for me to move my stones and other things around the house. The stone was by the TV in the family room. I hadn't moved it, though; it had slipped my mind after I heard Rachel bring through the information from the burgundy shorts. Now, as I wrote out the *Who are you to write a book?* inner dialogue I was having with myself, I found my composure and remembered I needed to move the stone. As I walked over to the TV stand and picked up the stone, I heard Rachel's text message tone. With the stone in hand I picked up my phone to read what she had to say. Her text read:

I was asking Josiah what he was looking for by the river? He says he is looking for a green stone.

I immediately took a picture of the stone – a Prasiolite, also known as a *Green Amethyst* – that I was holding in my hand. As I did, shivers embraced my being; I could feel liquid gold begin to drizzle through the puzzled areas of my heart.

I was filled with courage, as I heard my son so clearly:

"Snap out of it! I am here, Mom! Let's tell OUR story. Let's write a book!"

I pray my relationship with Josiah gives you peace, hope and a new way to experience your child in spirit.

This book is my journey – from giving birth and watching that life grow, to the nine adult years of holding my breath as I watched that life transform, evolve, and suspend, all at the same time. Silently screaming at the *"C" Monster* inside his body, to not take him from me, when a chance encounter with a tree, not the monster, became his portal through the translucent door, and the way we communicate between it.

My hope is my story offers you, "The Heart of *their* Mother," a peace in knowing that your child is still here.

I want you to journey through these pages with pen in hand and your soul wide open. Write down every time I say something that reminds you of your own experience and expand on that. Even the tiniest sign that left you wondering, *Is that my baby?* See what comes to you, and through you.

As you understand the "Sacred Alchemy of Josiah" and the synchronicities I have experienced, may you be able to gather the puzzle pieces of your story with your child, and gain a sense of peace in this pain from a higher perspective.

You are connected more than you know. Your connection to your child, your bond, is Love!

Those signs are not your imagination; they exist and will continue to do so. Pay attention, acknowledge even the subtlest hints, and then – Watch out, Mommaz – those are the moments when liquid gold will fill in the shredded tapestry of your entire being, weaving its way to reconstructing the person you now are. Bond to Bond. Heart to Heart. Your Spirit connected to theirs.

Tears still fall, they always will. Writing this book was a healing, layered with blankets of uncontrollable tears, almost drowning me from the weight of them. I miss Josiah more than my tattered tale can tell you, but I know he is with me. I know that he is speaking to me.

This book is evidence. And I know he aligns my heart with certainty to continue. There is nothing that could ever shake my faith in that. NOTHING!

This IS the Unimaginable. It has taken us from nowhere to now, here. Blank. Breathless. Everything unrecognizable. And from this point, you must redefine who you are. Because of them.

Hold your hearts steady, Sacred Mommaz. All we can do is continue, so continue with them. Honor them every day you live. Let your mind rest and know without a shadow of a doubt, your child is standing next to you, right this second.

I am You, and You are me... We vibrate to a frequency altered by the unimaginable we are present to now...

Josiah entered this world the same way he exited, With Me knowing Him!

Our bonds continue...

"Let the light show you the way and may love fill your lungs with every breath."

~ Josiah David

To My Mother

*E*arly in my life My Mother would tell me I needed to write a book. She seemed to think I had a "knack" for writing. While it was true, I could make *some* sense on paper, an entire BOOK!! I would tell her, "I Know Mom," never putting pen to paper except for the poetry and short stories she found so charming.

As I write these pages, I sense her reflection, as she too, witnessed two of her four children return to Spirit.

Never ever could I fathom in my unraveling state of mind, that I would fulfill my mother's wishes, "Because of Josiah!"

Here is to you My beautiful Mother. You showed me strength in sorrow. You taught me to hold my head up and continue, and during your tears, you remained my constant.

I Love You.

In 2004, my brother Eddie died of an overdose. He had struggled his whole life. When he left, I wrote this poem for my mother...

The Heart of His Mother

He was Challenged
She saw His Charm
He was Stubborn
She saw His Sensitivity
He was Unsteady
She saw His Strength
The Heart of His Mother

He knew Better
She looked for the Best
He was Difficult
She looked for something Different
He Hurt
She Hurt more
The Heart of His Mother

He is at rest
Will She Rest Now
He has No Pain
Will Her Pain End
He has Died
Yet He Lives
In "The Heart of His Mother"
There is No Greater Love
"The Heart of His Mother"

Who am I?
*I Am the **Heart** of Josiah's Mother*
Beauty, Strength & Healing,

Polished Through the Pain

October 2018

No one tells you how the story will end; like watching a movie, you guess, assume, and conjure up an outcome that makes the most sense to you. So many movies leave us puzzled, perplexed, and bewildered, wondering how the screenwriter could think the audience would leave the theater satisfied with such an ending. You know what I am talking about; the what-just-happened? That-ending-sucks-kind of movies.

Yet life smacks us with these endings to the stories we are living more often than we want to view; Instantly you look down and see your heart is in the palm of your hand, you are void of air, and you wonder how you will insert it back into its proper position.

This was me one year ago, when an instant message asking me for my phone number changed the space of my reality. A phone call to a hospital hundreds of miles away and a voice on the other end speaking the unimaginable: "Your son was in a motorcycle accident; we gave him CPR for an hour but ..."

BUT??? There is no *but*! Shut up, stop talking to me, you are not real, this is not the way this story ends!

As I turned into a mist in my kitchen, I unconsciously handed the tainted voice on the phone to my husband, and the vapor I had now become reappeared outside, screaming his name: "Josiah, Josiah,

Josiah, where are you, where are you??" Since I had no legs, the ground was my only refuge. Laboring to breathe, I could hear a crackling from my hand that now held my heart, shredded.

The earth had shifted, simultaneously expanding my understandings that had vanished.

Love began to arrive in the form of siblings, aunts, uncles, father and friends, each one entering with their hand dripping with the shreds of not only their hearts but mine as well. Love has a unique dialect in a crisis and had advised them to hold a piece of mine. As each one of my beautiful children, relatives and friends managed to find my mist, our shreds blended until only one heart could be felt – HIS!

One by one I gathered back the ribbons of my heart from theirs, this is my enigma and I would need every ribbon if I was going to survive this unimaginable alteration in the script and not just go with him, which momentarily teetered my thoughts.

How one day can alter perception like no other day has the possibility of doing, leaving you with more questions, and no answers.

What do I do with the tear-stained shreds that were once a heart, how do I reshape it and place it back in its proper position? What choice do you have when you *had* no choice?

All I had believed withered into the unstable earth my weakened bones now lay upon.

I am now unmolded clay on the Sculptor's wheel, but how do I mold and create the next part of my present moment when I am clay-less vapor? How do I surrender to the Sculptor to mold me and move me in the direction I will become, the creation that only dark despair creates?

Grief has a way of sliding through you like no other emotion, shape-shifting the current of your DNA.

I felt like a moment was too distant to wander to. I believed I was broken beyond human recognition, and that this was going to be the remainder of my existence.

When you are shredded, however that comes to be, you have a choice. You can absorb, digest, and become. Or, you can stay defeated, which silences the healing and secrets the re-scripting of this docudrama you are now living.

A friend asked me, "What is the gift he left you?", which challenged the alignment of my mind. So, I began to question the gift in the shreds, in the ribbons of my heart, in the vaporized clay. I asked myself, "What form do you choose to become, and how will you recalculate, reevaluate and respond to this act in your movie?" I am now in the scene where I am faced with life at its rawest expression of cruelty – at least this is my initial perception. This path feels wrong, blurred with deception. The earth is lying to me without words. If this is not how it is supposed to end, then I am not at the ending. I am at a pause. An intermission, where the actors realign and relationships redefine, including mine with Josiah...

And there it was! LOVE.

Love appeared again, now in the vexed eyes of my children!

"Will she stay, or will she go?"

And since there was no way I was leaving them, I could feel the two worlds merging.

How do I stay with him, and be here with them?

My breath now bleeding, I sang out:

"Josiah, it has been too many days, too many quiet moments. My labored breath awaits your voice, this void with no end, awaiting tears that perch my soul!"

With ink still wet and without warning, I heard him!

"Oh, Mother of this earth.

I am with you; I hold your heart from here,

stronger than I could when there; It is I, that perch your soul."

His ginormous Spirit was reminding me that he had me, that his presence had just changed form, that he was happy, healthy, healed, and whole now, and that he would guide my way, our way, and maybe yours as well.

I honestly cannot give you a timeframe in which I reappeared in my body. I am sure I am not all there now, and quite possibly I never will be. I like the place in-between, the merge. But what I have come to know is, I cannot be there unless I am *here*. Unless I live in Love, I won't be able to transmute this pain, which is Love on the deepest level.

We have all loved and lost; we have all carried the shreds and gathered the ribbons.

To say I am grateful doesn't feel right, but it doesn't feel wrong either. Just the mere fact that he chose me. That I had him in my body, and that his magical being loved me! I am humbled. Gratitude seems too faint an expression.

If you were to ask me, "Raina, if you knew this was part of the script would you say yes again?" I would answer, "Yes! A million times, YES! Yes, to loving him. Yes, to knowing him. Yes, to the privilege of being his mother. Yes, to the magic that is Josiah!" And as my tears stain these pages, I say, "Yes! For the gift he gave me was himself, and I am beyond grateful."

Now I have form again, and I am being sculpted into something other than what I once was. My ribbons lay upon the sculpture differently, yet they are uniquely still mine –repurposed. And though it may take beyond this lifetime to see the polished performance from this movie, to see the glossy finish, I willingly say:

Yes, polish me Spirit, polish me Angels, polish me Josiah.

Let me be Love, let me be light and let me honor you in my movie, because it's not over.

To love is our greatest gift, to "Be Love" is even greater.

Will you gather the ribbons, will you embrace your enigma, and will you rise with me and call on love to show you the gift? There are some pains so great that others fade in comparison. Choose to be polished, for even if you can't see that you shine, someone else can. I can.

My Heart, My Soul, My Spirit, My Life will never be the same.

It will be Stronger.

Because of Josiah.

JOSIAH
(Three years old)

I bite his cheeks his ears his nose,
I have to bite him that's how it goes

His little face I cannot resist, without him,
I would not exist

He holds my hair, he sucks his thumb,

My little boy, the prize I won

I don't believe that it is chance

He chose through me, this life to dance

He heals my heart when it is broke

He makes me laugh, He likes to joke

Thank you, G-d, for my little man

I'll guide him to Spirit the best I can

I don't think it will be hard, He's guided by love

He is my guard.

A rainbow of color he brightens each day

Any amount of treasure, I'd gladly pay

To have such an essence, enter to be

To watch him unfold, through His eyes I see.

~Raina Irene, 1991

Part I

The Early Years

"*Love all of everything. Then, throw it into the wind and watch it dance into the sunrise. It is a brand-new day to love.*"

~ *Josiah David*

Form

" *F*orm? Do I have to become form again? I like it here, why must I go?" squawked Josiah with understandable apprehension.

"She needs you; they need you," whorled an Ethereal voice.

"Must I stay long?"

"No, this time will be a shorter visit. One that will teach you, to teach them, about us. You will light the way for others. It won't be easy this time, Josiah, not for you, not for your mother, not for anyone."

"My mother?" His vibrational laughter turned to robust joy. "Oh yes, I want to be with her again! This incarnate, she will be my mother?"

"Yes, and this time you will be her guide."

"OH!" he exclaimed, vibrating now in dance, "This will be fun."

"Yes, Josiah, it will be fun. You will be filled with extraordinary talents and abilities, and because of this, you will be in constant need of humbling. You will be able to remember an ancient wisdom, and it will come to you through a horrific incident that will change the course of your life."

"I am going to be talented, wise and humble," he mused, reverencing at this idea, "I think I can handle that!"

"You might not like it as much as you think once it occurs."

3

"Well, you said I didn't have to stay long this time...?"

"Yes, I did say that. But you need to realize that this journey comes with heartache, as all lifetimes do. This one in particular will create a ripple unlike some of your other lifetimes. This one will be your last. You will not need to visit earth again in human form, unless you choose. That is why it will be so intense. It's the realization for you, Josiah."

The Ethereal paused. "Josiah? You are quiet now. You look apprehensive."

"My mother, my mother. I have never had to leave her this way. How can we do this to my mother?" Josiah cried as he wiped translucent tears from his eyes and held them to the amethyst ray that illuminated his chest.

"Josiah, in this lifetime she is being equipped. She will witness her own mother respond to the same journey. She is in her process to the next awakening. And Josiah, she said yes. She said she would do anything for you. She is the one who has already named you Josiah. She is waiting for you!"

That is all he needed to hear, and I was pregnant.

Birth

Josiah is my third and last-born child. It is true, there was an ethereal voice that told Josiah's father, Mitchell, and I that we would have a son named Josiah David. The first time I heard the name Josiah I was a young

4

girl in Sunday school. There was the wonderful King David and then not one good king until King Josiah arrived on the scene. I am fairly sure that sparked a knowing that I already had a son named Josiah. Mitchell and I wanted children immediately and started talking about names even before we had a baby on the way. I already had my girl's name since I was thirteen years old. I had met a Valerie in one of my junior high classes. As she introduced herself to me, her name rolled out of her mouth like flowers. It was just the most beautiful name I had ever heard. So, a girl's name was not up for negotiation. The name Josiah felt like it fell out of the sky to us, right along with David. We were convinced Josiah would arrive first. We just knew it.

Two months before I became pregnant, I had a dream. It was very vivid. I was in the hospital; I had just given birth to a girl, and I heard the name Valerie. I woke up sure I was pregnant with my daughter, but another month would pass before I actually became pregnant. As my due date approached, I began to think again about the name Josiah, which stirred up a fair amount of restlessness. How could this baby be a boy when the dream I'd had of a daughter was so real? I had not had an ultrasound (I didn't with any of my pregnancies), so there was still a 50/50 chance my dream was inaccurate. Even if I was carrying a boy, I knew this wasn't Josiah.

One day, I was chatting with another pregnant mom; her due date was coming up quicker than mine. "Raina, I am ping-ponging between the names Scott and Jeremy."

Jeremy! As soon as my ears heard that name, I had

the same experience I'd had when I met my friend Valerie all those years ago. But instead of flowers coming out of her mouth, it was hammers, bikes and fishing poles. At that moment, I knew I was carrying Jeremy.

One year later, I shut my eyes to rest while Jeremy slept beside me. I had another baby dream. Like that earlier dream, I had just given birth, this time to a boy named Josiah. Yet the scenery was different. In this dream, I was not in a hospital. I was at home. One month later, I was pregnant, I thought for sure with Josiah. We had moved to Washington State and my new friends were eager to share their wisdom and birth experiences. Bronwyn caught my attention as she shared about her third homebirth. I listened intently and realized she was describing my dream and guiding my direction.

On a snowy Saturday morning in February, I entered the exact scene of my dream... except it was not Josiah, but my redheaded Valerie who appeared. She looked exactly as she had in my first baby dream. My mom had flown to Washington to witness the birth, and after Mitchell and I checked every inch of Valerie's beauty, he placed her into Mom's arms, sealing their bond. Redhead to redhead.

What is up, I wondered, with my dreams showing me my children in non-chronological order? And where is Josiah?

Mitchell and I agreed that we would space the next baby just a little further out. Maybe three years, instead of two.

I should have been more aware a year and a half later when I had my third baby dream. This time I had delivered a boy. I could see him as clear as day, but there was no name attached to this baby as there had been in both of the other dreams. Dreamt of a girl, had a boy. Dreamt of a boy, had a girl. Was I going to be pregnant with another girl?

I thought I still had six months, but – surprise! – guess I wasn't in charge after all. We had been away at Mitchell's grandmothers house for Thanksgiving and, not thinking there would be any, "you know, and well, there was, and I had no protection with me. The only alternative, other than rolling over and going to sleep, was the "withdrawal method," which is no guarantee, especially when your baby-to-be has been conversing with "The Ethereal" and hears you are waiting for him.

One morning, I walked into the bathroom where Mitchell was getting ready for the day. I had been feeling just a bit off since our Thanksgiving getaway.

"You're pregnant!" he blurted out.

"What? No!" I squeaked, hoping he was joking.

"You're pregnant, I can tell. I see it in your face!"

I walked to the mirror and examined my face. What the what? I could see what he was seeing. There was something different in my aura.

I began a continuous plea to this Ethereal: *Please let this be Josiah.* I had been pregnant; nursed Jeremy for a year; immediately became pregnant again and nursed Valerie. The third time had to be a charm, because I was kind of over being pregnant. My dream showed me a boy. If this were a girl, I would have to become pregnant again. Not that it would have been the end of the world to have a fourth child, there was just something that felt right about three. In the middle of my mental quandary, I knew it was him. I felt a calm peace, even in the unknowing.

I knew this was Josiah.

But I tell you: he really did not want to enter. He had meant what he said in the ethers – "Do I have to become form again? I like it here. Why must I go?" – and now he was going to put off his arrival as long as possible.

My pregnancy was easy and, at the same time, unnerving. For the first four months I was on high alert that this baby wanted an early exit. Continual issues left me aflutter; until he settled into his new *in utero* form. The day prior to his birth, I woke up just before midnight, my body doing things it had not done in my previous labors. Those labors were a beautiful array of non-stop pains, so much so that my awareness to push was erratic. Josiah, however, was taking his own sweet time. It wasn't a hard labor or a long labor, but he was still apprehensive. He did not want to arrive. One-minute contraction. Three minutes in between. It was the most mind-boggling sensation as he waited patient-ly for three minutes in my birth canal. Push. Pause. *"I am just going to hang out in here, Mom."* Push. Pause. *"Ethereal, do I have to be born?"* Push. Pause. *"Fine, fine, I know! She is waiting for me!"* push.

Jeremy cut the cord; Valerie, just two and a half years old, had her arms out, ready to receive her baby brother, who at this point was still insisting he did not want to take in the full breath of this lifetime. (Thank goodness for my exhaustion, which gave me some distance from knowing he was struggling to breathe). The midwife administered oxygen, and, in the pre-dawn hours of August 19, 1988, his soul finally stopped resisting his new form and joined us in this, his next theater, as Josiah.

The Early Years, How Do I Write About Them?

This part of the story is uncooperative, vexing and agonizing. As I attempted to write it, I went blank, as if the memories had fallen into some sort of void.

As my mind continued its futile search, I too seemed to fall into the abyss. Completely deprived of memory. "What were those early years like?" I kept asking myself. "Why is it that I can remember some parts of this lifetime and others seem vague, as if they were a dream?"

Had the channels to my memories shattered when my heart did?

I look at the calendar and realize I am searching for memories on my father's birthday, which is ten days shy of Josiah's birthday. This is the second one I will succumb to without my son.

What were *my* early years like? I rotate backwards through my mind, questioning myself, wishing my Dad were here with me. Ever the quiet adviser and listener, he always believed I would make the right choice, even when he knew, deep down, that I would not. He would let his headstrong daughter fall, knowing that if she learned on her own, she would eventually make the choice he knew was best. Always reminding me, "You got this, Raina; you always figure it out. You are the overseer of your own destiny."

But today, I have no destiny. No direction. And not one memory.

I decided the best way to recall these memories was to look at them. Pictures! I was particularly proud of myself. I thought I was on the right access road toward the details of mine and Josiah's youth. Holy cow was I wrong! I am not the scrapbook, everything-in-albums kind of girl. I am the everything-in-boxes-and-bins-and-maybe-someday-I-will-organize-this-mess (and yeah, that will never happen) kind of girl. Let me give you a visual. I pulled out four bins from the closet. The giant bins from Walmart that you can hide an entire world in, each one representing the same as the next. The different stages of my life melding and blending with everyone else's... All there in each box; each picture jolting me backwards and forwards and sideways. Each picture holding stories and memories that smothered me with every emotion possible. I had become Alice, rapidly falling down the rabbit hole to the Mad Hatter's table. Or was I the Mad Hatter himself?

Either way, I was deep within this rabbit hole, with the four bins now emptied on the guestroom floor, the piles of pictures, organized according to face, surrounding me. There was Mom and Dad's pile; my younger sister Sheri's pile; Jeremy's pile; Valerie's pile; my stepson "bonus child," Brian's pile. Nephews; nieces; grandchildren; etcetera. You get the scene I had tunneled down. And of course, there was Josiah's pile.

I was surrounded by a lifetime I had created and shelved. All the lessons learned, and unlearned, and relearned surrounded me, without an inch of carpet I could slither through to get out of the mayhem and the magic. What the hell had I just done to myself? I let these pictures, this magical mess, rest on the floor for days, as if they had become a part of it. Which made me even more entangled in the webs that lined my rabbit hole.

With one word – "Dad!" – I begged my father-in-Spirit for his quiet advice.

"My goodness, daughter, put everything back. One thing at a time."

Seriously! It took me days to figure that out.

I knew I had made a small dent in the picture-organizing process, but far from the pride of anything that launched real order. I took ziplocked bags and gathered each face, save Josiah's, and sealed them into their own container. I then stacked the bins of my memories upon themselves and nested them back into the closet. I thought I would function better now with only his pile. Wrong all over again...

All those pictures I had looked at and nested back into their proper place were not the memories I was void of. They were the lives and loves of all that is still here, and of those that were not my child.

Once more I encircled myself with Josiah's pictures. There he was. As a small child. His birthday parties. His circus antics. Graduation. Disney. College, and his boho hippie charisma, hypnotizing me.

Now just days away from his birthday. My madness. My heartache. And my mind was breaking down even more.

I felt like I was in labor, with every cell in my body remembering when he was within me, getting ready to enter this world. My breath weakened as I focused on what was happening, crying as the intensity crescendoed!

How am I going to write about his life when I cannot see it? When the picture screen will not materialize anything but white noise and cloudy graphics?

I had to walk away... hesitant... fearing I may never be able to tell you who he is.

Then one morning something shifted, I walked in my healing room and said, "No more fear, and no more mystery memories."

What shifted?

A dream! That morning, Josiah was in my dream.

How I remembered the dream after I had woken up. Poured my coffee and spoke with my seven-year-old grandson Gavin on the phone, blew my mind, but I did.

During my morning meditation, coffee still in hand, my dream came into view.

I was at my house, but it did not look like the home I live in now. Friends were over; however, I was not sure who they were. I asked them to follow me into what seemed like a den that had toffee-colored wooden cabinets. I opened one of the cabinet doors to show my visitors the mementos I had in there. They were all Josiah's things. Knickknacks. It was a corner cabinet, and this door was smaller than the rest of the doors. I had my back to my guests as I pointed out the thises and the thats. I did not realize Josiah was standing behind me until he spoke. "It is so small!" he announced. I turned around and there he was. In the center of our friends. "This is only part of it, Josiah!" I exclaimed to him. "Let me show you the rest. My entire home is a sanctuary for you!"

Then I woke up.

I wrote down the dream, then immediately began to question it. Why was he there watching me? What was he trying to tell me? I focused on the dream – my questions and the answer. In absolute pure fluidity, I knew. He was pouring liquid lyrics through the cloudy graphics. The white noise faded, and I could hear him.

"Mom, why are you looking at what is in the small cabinet? The thises and the thats?"

"There was so much more," I reminded him, *"My entire home is a sanctuary for you!"*

"Exactly!" he continued, *"you are looking instead of seeing. You are my mom. No one knows more about her children than their mother. August is over. Begin again!"*

Oh, he is an insistent child. Through these twenty-two months he has been physically gone, he has still been here, and once more he pushes me forward...

"Everyone has a voice; they just have to find it."

~ Josiah David

Begin Again

Now that I am on the other side of his birthday month, the mayhem and Josiah's dream direction, memories have returned. I begin again.

I have always been confident that Josiah came here with the intention of doing this lifetime on his own terms.

Straight out of the womb, he began entertaining us with his never-ending array of facial expressions. Ridiculous comedic remarks wrapped up in insight and humility.

He knew he had heard me calling from the ethers, so he stayed close, using my fine, wavy brown hair as a blanket. He would wrap it ever so neatly around his thumb as he sucked it. I don't have the long  locks of a hair model, so I found it quite unique that he found comfort in just a few strands of hair. As he grew older, he would stop in the middle of playing to wander over to me and grab my hair, quickly wrap it around his thumb, and pop it into his mouth for a moment of connection before dashing off again. Of course, I would drop whatever I was doing, I loved it. I loved how connected he was to me.

Beauty, Strength & Healing

When my children were ten, eight and six, their father and I did what crushes the heart of a family: we divorced.

My three children and I began to redefine who we had always been.

As heartbreaking as divorce can be, it will also illuminate strengths you weren't aware you had. This was happening to my children as well. Each one of our roles were being defined within our new family dynamic. As I was watching them, I could see they were also watching me.

Differently yet uniquely the same.

Jeremy is my outdoorsman. It was hard to contain him. He liked to get on his bike with his friends and ride. Now, he began to pause at the door before he would leave. He never asked me anything verbally; he would look at me and say telepathically, *Are you okay, Mom? I will stay if you want me to and give you strength!* There were days I needed him to stay. But a ten-year-old, especially a heartbroken one, needs his wings. So, I would say, "I'm okay, handsome. Be back before dark. You *are* the Strength of my life!"

Valerie stayed close to me. We would do what moms and daughters do. Valerie sees the beauty in everything. She sees color in vivid proportion. It was like she was magically embroidering my heart with her poems, and beautiful flowers she would color for me. And though her own heart was crushed, she constantly reminded me that there was still beauty to see. And she made sure to decorate my world with that beauty.

Like his siblings, Josiah had a keen sense of when I was hurting, crying, or upset. Like clockwork, he would waltz in the house and begin speaking to me in gibberish. I would respond in that same gibberish. It became our secret language. He would make one of those facial expressions that would crack up a stranger, then walk over to me, grab my hair and wrap it around his thumb. My pain would evaporate, my mind would calm, and healing would flood my heart.

I had always strived to look through my children's eyes and now they were showing me something new. They were teaching me the true definition of beauty, strength and healing. Not only were they teaching it to me; they had become the essence of it as well.

Oochie

Josiah was three when we bought him his first drum set and guitar. He took flute in school, played soccer and ran in marathons with his fourth-grade teacher that he insisted I do so with him.

He had a keen eye for nature and drew pictures from an almost architectural perspective. He had his own perception of the world and his abilities to contribute to it were never ending.

It only took one facial scolding, when I was late to get him, for me to learn how important time was to him. So, to soften his brow, I broke out in a rap song, "Oochawad nada haad, bitty botty boo, Oochawad nada haad, I love you!" Yup, it has a tune. Don't even try to sound it out. There is no spelling for the words I used. I started calling him "Oochie," and/or, "Ooochies the baby." Which turned into another song.

When he was ten, Josiah walked into the family room and announced, "I am going to be ten, so I am going to stop sucking my thumb!"

I felt faint. Of course, he was going to stop sucking his thumb at some point. But what about my hair? What about those moments? To top it off, this declaration coincided with his need for me to cease calling him Oochie. This was a tiny jolt to my mommy ego. A couple weeks had passed, and Josiah overheard me talking to one of my friends on the phone. I was lamenting. Telling her how I missed those moments. As soon as I hung up the phone. Josiah walked over to me, grabbed my hair and wrapped it around his thumb. Then he looked at me and smiled. I knew this was the last hurrah. That he was giving me "a gift and a goodbye" to this particular connection we had shared. I hugged him with everything I had. Kissed him way too many times for a ten-year-old and told him, "Thank you." As he walked away,

I sat there, amazed at the depth of understanding he had.

His Essence

Josiah loved the ocean. I am not sure if it was the first time he smelled the salt air, dipping his tiny toes in the waves and hunting for shells in the sand? Or the many adventures that one of his elementary school friend's family took him on that sealed this emotion. But early on he knew it cleansed his soul. It was only natural, then, that he, his father, and Jeremy would learn to scuba dive and explore its depths. When Jeremy was twenty-one and Josiah was seventeen, the two of them headed to South America for a scuba adventure – brothers on an expedition of a lifetime. Lordy, Lordy, I thought this was going to give me a coronary. My two sons roaming the wilds of the unknown. But I also knew this was going to be epic for both of them. Jeremy assured me he would watch out for Josiah.

"You two watch over each other!" I said in a calm panic, "I was once twenty-one!" It was in that moment, that I truly understood what my poor mother must have felt, when I jumped on a plane to Italy when I was Jeremy's age. She must have held her breath until I arrived home, as I did with them.

The ocean never failed Josiah, and neither did the desert or the mountains. He was well-versed in the atmospheres, knowing each climate had something to offer that the others could not. Luckily, we lived in an area of California that sits smack in the middle of all these climates, with the beach, the mountains and the desert just a short forty-five minutes in any direction.

And in each of these directions Josiah made friends, loads of them. He had a way about him. Rooted deep within Josiah was the keen sense to know when someone was hurting or needed a kind word. And he didn't have to know them that well to see it. He had a way of hearing you from your perspective and interjecting his wisdom without making you feel wrong. He was generous, sometimes to a fault. He would give you what he needed or wanted because you needed it more. I witnessed his gratitude for everything and everyone that shared a part in his world. Josiah wasn't interested in finding the popular friend. He was looking for true friends. Soul friends. And he found them, or should I say, they found him.

Josiah's charm and charisma were seriously infectious.

Women loved him. And not just women his own age, women of *any* age. My friends wanted to steal him from me, literally begging me to take him home. And he loved women, not because he was a womanizer but because he was interested in a woman's perspective, knowing that there was a yin and a yang to everything, that every perspective was important. He listened with ears of consideration and eyes of interest, and with the deepest part of friendship and trust.

Circus

When he was fourteen, soccer ceased.

We were gifted tickets to see the great American Y circus at our local YMCA. Josiah left there petitioning me to enroll him in the next season.

That was it. His creative juices were turned on. He was in his element. He was thriving. Mastering juggling, the unicycle, the German wheel, and the Chinese pole. I watched, mesmerized, when he suspended himself straight out from the pole, as if he were a flag. I cried as he flew above the crowd, wrapped up in red ribbons like an Angel above me.

Then there was Clowning. The faces and antics were hilarious. He was just so funny. He loved the costumes, the laughter and awe of the crowd. And the applause;

the applause warmed his soul, took his breath away, and enlivened his spirit. Confirming to him he was in his element.

Josiah's charm infiltrated a room with his light that entered your heart. His distinctive laugh is unforgettable!

It was his circus years that taught him to be truly present in his body. It disciplined his mind. Performing gave him a peace he hadn't realized he was missing. He was becoming more aware of himself.

His thoughts were shifting.

One afternoon he unburdened himself to me in a way that blew my mind. "I have spent so much of my young life quiet, letting people say unkind things and acting like it just rolled off my back. But it didn't roll off!"

"What?" I asked in shock.

"I know none of what these people do are because of me, so, I can't really blame them. But I *have* taken it all in. I observe people and they deeply influence my mood, even if I am not a part of the situation. Like a sponge I sit through life, absorbing energies that are not mine!"

I was dumbfounded. My empathic child, now learning how to protect himself from how others, who he never named, had impacted him. He went on to tell me, "The circus is my escape. When I perform, nothing else matters. My true self steps up to say hello, and shine." He knew how it made him feel to perform, yet he wrestled with feeling he was not doing his best.

I think this is where that humbling emotion the Ethereal spoke of before his birth would get filtered. His talents were endless, but he could not always see it. I had no idea why he was so hard on himself; I was the mother who praised my children for four right answers on a test and dismissed the five they got wrong. (Jeremy often tells me I wear rose-colored glasses.) Yet I had been hard on myself while they were growing up. Had Josiah heard my unthoughtful rhythm? I was careful not to spew my own insecurities out around them, but they are mine and I am theirs. We were all one, traveling together through this life. How could they have not picked up on my bullshit? I felt called out. Was this my fault? It was time for my energy to shift with his, and for his, for all of them.

Josiah was quick to pick up on my thoughts. "Mom, it's not your fault. You have always been my biggest fan!"

Seriously? Had he read my mind again??

Now that he had this off his chest, a relief settled in him. He took a deep breath and thanked me, as if I had done something miraculous. I had not, he had. He had given me the gift of his truth, and his forgiveness.

Disney

Given his love of the circus and all it entailed, it was natural that he chose to study theater design in college. He then landed his dream job at Disney, humoring people in the parade of dreams. Dressed up as the five of diamonds on the Alice in Wonderland float. Jumping on and off the trampoline, gracefully flying, landing and dancing the dream of his youth.

Until...

Part II

The Evolution of Josiah

"*Strive for what you want to be good at. Love that you are beautiful and worthy of your own life. You are a bright light that never fails. Love yourself deeper and you will see how you are beyond enough.*"

~*Josiah David*

I See Fire

*O*n August 17th, two days before his twentieth birthday, Josiah came out from Orange County to perform circus antics for Jeremy's son's birthday.

One of his non-circus acts was breathing fire. I was not a fan of this act. It was cool, but I was not too keen on the fumes. Josiah loved it, though. He was quite good at it, and it was a crowd pleaser. After his fire-breathing act, he began struggling to breathe. He believed he had inhaled some of the gases and it would pass. Let me remind you of his entrance at birth. His lungs were always a bit of a challenge. So, you understand my dismay at this trick.

After the party, Josiah and I went to the movies for *his* birthday. He continued to struggle but reassured me he was fine. I didn't want him to drive back to Orange County, but he insisted.

"Call me as soon as you get home!"

"I will Mom, I promise." *You worry too much,* he thought but did not speak. It was in that facial expression I saw. As promised, he called when he arrived home, then again at midnight. This time He was upset. His lungs would not clear. I told him to go to the hospital immediately. He was apprehensive.

"But Mom, we don't have insurance right now!"

"Who cares. Go anyway!"

Ten minutes later he called again, this time from the car. I asked him if one of his roommates was with him. There were three of them. Surely one would go!

"No one should go to the emergency room alone!" I cried, somehow keeping the echo of fear from my voice. "Go back upstairs and ask one of them."

With me still on the phone, he walked back upstairs, and in his Josiah way, poked his head in the screenless kitchen window and asked, "Who'll go with me?"

I heard Paul say, "I will," then I fell back into a feeble attempt to sleep.

3:30 AM.

The phone rattled me awake a few hours later.

"Mom, I got some good news, and I got some bad news. Which do you want first?"

"Funny boy. You still got to be funny!" I held my breath and muttered, "Tell me both."

In an unalarming voice he said, "The good news is I have a mild case of pneumonia..."

"And the bad news?" sprinted immediately out from my voice box.

"The bad news is they found a mass in my chest. You need to come here in the morning and go with me to see a specialist."

With the word *mass* echoing into a massive tidal wave of fear, that I kept deep within, I told him I would be there first thing in the morning. That I would take care of it.

At that moment I thought I could. "Get some sleep, son. I will be there shortly."

What in the world just happened? Put down the phone from your ear, Raina. He's okay. He is not on the phone anymore.

That thought was silenced by the reverberating waves of tears waterfalling down my face. I collected my legs, familiarized them on the carpet and, in a haze, wandered to my grandkids' playroom. There, among the toys, was the collection of monkeys I had given Josiah over the years. There were two monkeys that my friend Lisa, one of the friends who wanted to steal him, had given him. Moe and Joe. I dug unconsciously through the pile of monkeys until I found Joe. Making my way back down the hallway, I landed on my pillow and cried myself into a stupor.

Dr. X

Awakened once more by the screaming telephone, my heart left my chest. I answered to hear my daughter Valerie saying, "Mom, can you come? I have a flat tire!" Analyzing this next crisis. I shifted back to my earlier phone call from Josiah. *Or had that been a dream?*

Then it became clear.

"No, Beauty, call your dad." I told her of Josiah's phone call and what I needed to do. I was about to tell her to call her dad again but stopped mid-sentence and said instead, "Call Jeremy. I need to call your dad."

I dialed Mitchell. It rang only once, but it felt like he would never answer. The ringing so loud in my ear. A shallow "hello" shot through me; then, as my words began to fall from my mouth and onto my children's father's ear, my panicked heart continued to unravel, one thread at a time.

I drove to Mitchell's, handed him my keys and into the deepest unknown we traveled towards our son. The specialist knew nothing. He confirmed there was a mass, but it was debatable. He told us Josiah either needed a surgeon to remove the mass, or an oncologist.

Oncologist? Is this a word from another language? I could not comprehend what he just said (the scene is still a little hazy in my mind). I was bewildered, shocked and trying my best to look strong on the outside for my child. We then drove to Josiah's to call this "so-called oncologist."

My thoughts were weak as I composed myself to be the pillar Josiah required me to be.

We stayed that night with Josiah and his three roommates. Thank goodness he lived with men as funny as him. It made this night bearable. We woke early, forced something that resembled food down and headed to the oncologist's office.

As we drove there, my thoughts appeared dis-figured. I had already dismissed the possibility that we needed an oncologist. Josiah needed surgery. Period. They were going to take this intruder out of his body. And that would be that. The dictator of my inner voice continued... *And there will be flowers, and butterflies, and mystical creatures following him.* I saw his healing as I wanted it. As we pulled to a stop at the office, I neatly boxed up my thoughts, as I was spliced back to the present moment.

We entered the chilling reception area, my eyes

taking in the scene. Patients sitting with the same look of wonder, anticipating or awaiting the medicine of hope prescribed to kill the beast inside them. Their companions holding their hand in deep love and support. And fear.

At this moment I was most definitely the weakest link in this group. I ushered Mitchell to handle check-in so I could sit with Josiah. We waited, my hand holding his. Reassuring him, all will be okay, while inwardly begging my fears to stay asunder.

"Josiah, you can come back now," the nurse bellowed, her words like invisible darts to my ears. We entered the examining room and waited some more, shortened breath mixed with hope as prayers escaped towards heaven. The doctor – we'll call him Dr. X – entered, his energy heightened. I sensed this was part of his persona. His delivery piercing and unkind. He describes where the beast was and what we needed to do, immediately, or Josiah would die.

Holy cow, Doc, take it down a notch so we can properly digest the cruelty you are delivering. Aware that we have no insurance, he softens and tells us to go back to "his" hospital and he will take care of us. He will get Josiah set up with proper coverage, run all the appropriate tests to get a full conclusion.

My last memory of that visit is walking out of the examining room in high gear, leaving the boys in the dust, straight to the parking lot so I could bow to the searing of my soul in solitude.

Pocketed

The ride back to Josiah's was a blur. Our minds are magnificent creations with hidden pockets. These pockets keep the records we cannot familiarize ourselves with.

We had no idea this was going to turn into the longest most dreadful outing to date. We told Josiah we would be right back. We were going to go home and pack a bag so we could stay with him. We settled him at home, his eyes speaking volumes, as he asked us to hurry.

The ride back to pack was abstract. I remember a nonstop conversation with Mitchell, but what was said? It is in one of those pockets. I do remember Mitchell and I coming out of our talking blackout to find we were on an unfamiliar freeway, though thankfully leading us in the right direction. I dropped him off and headed to my solitude to pack.

My anxiety was sprouting in all directions. I wrestled with the staccato thoughts in my head. I knew I better make a list of what I needed, or I would never be able to pull off the packing job. But then my daughter called to check in and, within her "hello," I began to unknot. Hysteria erupted, with words that could not possibly line up with my reality, then I tell her I don't know what to pack.

"Mom, you need a toothbrush," she said calmly.

I looked. "I have it, it's in the suitcase, Beauty."

"You need underwear."

"Got it, Beauty."

"You need this, you need that."

All was in my suitcase. My alter ego had already packed everything I would need.

I was ready to go, but far from ready for what lay ahead.

The Cold Abyss

In a tailspin I embraced the steering wheel of my white Honda Accord. The fifteen-minute drive back to Mitchell's? Pocketed.

Thank goodness, even after fourteen years apart, we are still in sync enough for me to once again, hand him the keys and slide into the passenger side for the ride that was about to alter every aspect of my/our existence.

As we arrived back at Josiah's apartment we chose to relax. I wanted him to feel calm. I needed to feel calm. We had decided we would go to the hospital in the morning. We all needed rest. We needed to be as clear as possible. I tried to secret my fears from Josiah. That is hard to do when your son knows you so well.

"Mom, sleep in my bed with me!" He knew what I needed. I needed him and I needed him to need me.

The night was long. Sleep was not available. Not to any of us. But I laid quietly, hoping he would rest.

Morning arrived too quickly, after the longest night of my life.

Now we were off to the cold abyss they call a hospital. Like an arrival committee at the airport, this doctor was there to greet us. We got Josiah settled in, and Dr. X began a succession of tests. I must say he certainly was thorough. For ten days he kept Josiah in the hospital. Blood work. Biopsy in his chest, and bone marrow test. The medicine before the bone marrow test made Josiah loopy. He decided to enjoy the drug and tell us jokes, turning his clown on for our entertainment. Then, Dr. X shoed us out. We sat on the floor in the hallway outside the door until it was over. The waiting room was just too far. Dr. X looked at us like we were crazy.

I think in times like these, a supernatural phenomenon happens. Most people call it *autopilot,* but it's much bigger than that. It is a supernatural grace. That feels better to me. It's a supernatural superpower given to parents. And a special dose reserved for *the heart of the mother.* I needed that dose because at the end of all these tests, all the poking and prodding, this is what we were told:

"I am now positive about what your son has. It is stage 2 Hodgkin's lymphoma. Here is your one and only option or he will die."

Wait, what? Did I not send enough prayers through my tears? Had I not been heard? I am confused. This is not true! What is being verbalized to my ears? This man is insane! A fraud! May lightning strike him for this blasphemy!

Josiah's Choice

We took in all the information the doctor had spewed on us.

Josiah decided he wanted to start school before he started chemotherapy. It was late August, and he was about to start his third year of college. He wanted to get himself acclimated to this part of his journey before he took on what the doctor deemed "his only treatment." He asked me to call the doctor to advise him of his thoughts. *Why me?* I thought. Remember, I am the weakest link in this triangle. Yet I agreed. I rang the doctor's office. The receptionist answered. I told her how we would like to wait a bit while Josiah started his school year.

She immediately asked me to hold, and within seconds, Dr. X announced himself. He began yelling at me, asking me, "Didn't I help you? Wasn't I a god to your son? He is going to die if he doesn't start chemo!"

I tried to explain, "He just wanted to start school, it's just a few weeks," but Dr. X berated me. I hung up the phone completely unhinged and called Mitchell. Mitchell is the one you call when there is a threat, or a tough situation and you need a bellowing voice. He will set it straight. This doctor might have thought he could bully me, but there was no way he was going to bully Mitchell.

We did not go back to see Dr. X. This injured Josiah's Spirit. Why was this doctor being so unreasonable?

Our time in the hospital had also given us pause to research natural alternatives to chemo after Dr. X vomited this on us. "This type of chemo can make you sterile. You should probably freeze your sperm!"

Josiah reached for my hand immediately, his deep brown eyes piercing mine. Whether he wanted children or not was not the point, he was clairvoyantly telling me. It was that they were taking away his option to have them. And honestly, it was at that moment I knew chemotherapy was never going to be part of this process.

Now that we had successfully removed Dr. X from this equation, we (or should I say he? No, we) were wide open for the transformation that was deliberately and rapidly occurring.

Josiah was on a quest. He began to search out everything he could about what had manifested in his body, and why. What he deemed would be the roadmap he would take to eliminate it. Although this map was completely unmarked. He had his drawing apparatus out and ready to draw. A pioneer to the new world he would conquer, road by road.

Nancy's Vision

That first year after the diagnosis was filled with many twists and turns, most of which I could not have anticipated. There was one, however, that I was warned about and didn't want to acknowledge. It came from my friend Nancy, who is a gifted shaman, during one of our monthly trades. Nancy always receives the most incredible messages from beyond and this time was no different.

"Josiah has something to tell you," she said, "He is apprehensive to your reaction."

I could hear in her voice she was confident in the information as well as puzzled by it. My response was quick and sure. "That is ridiculous! Josiah isn't scared to tell me anything! Are you sure that is what you are hearing?"

She was.

"What could he have to tell me that is worse than what I have already become aware of? What could be worse than hearing your son has the "C word?" (I was still unable to say that word.) Not to mention the several curveballs he'd thrown me since the diagnosis.

Nancy paused to question her guides once more. Her soft voice spoke again, "I'm still getting there is something, it feels strong."

We finished our evening, and I took in all my beautiful friend had to say, except that Josiah was apprehensive to tell me something. All my kids know that they can tell me anything, and they do. Josiah had no fear of his mother, so why on earth would I be warned?

Two days later, Josiah called. "Mom, I have something to tell you and I don't think you are going to like it, but I am doing it anyway!"

Okay, Nancy's guides, thanks for the warning I dismissed! I quickly told Josiah about my conversation with Nancy two days earlier. "She said you had something to tell me that you were apprehensive about!"

Extremely amused, Josiah continued, "I am moving

out to Joshua tree to live on a commune of sorts!"

Apparently, the gods had been right to warn me. I should have listened.

"You are going to do what? No! Why do you want to?"

"Mom, I knew you weren't going to like this, but it is the way I need to go. It is part of my healing!"

The first road had been drawn. Any writing style I had to help draw on this map were quickly removed from my hand. He was determined to find his way. I knew from that moment that my drawing apparatus was going to have to be invisible ink. And only if I could get to that map. Draw. Hopefully he would see the energy of my ink and put his own pen to it.

Sandwich Cookie

Having your child diagnosed with anything more than the common cold is grueling. A high fever smothers your heart with despair, never mind cancer. Who came up with such a horrible word, that summons fear so great it defies human interpretation? Cancer is a zodiac sign, damn it, not something that has the potential to swallow his life. And mine.

I felt his diagnosis so deeply that my own body weakened. It began four months almost to the day after he decided chemo was not the answer. Not that I wanted him to do chemotherapy. I did not want any of this. And my body reported the evidence to me.

Not only was Josiah on my heart, but my mother, now in her nineties, needed my time more often than she wanted to admit. Keeping her feeling independent and in control of her own destiny, was merging with Josiah's harrowing diagnosis, and it was taking its toll on me.

My inner self realized this before my outer self-had time to gather the information.

I had become the very thin icing of this sandwich cookie.

The weight of my son's diagnosis was so heavy that both my shoulders froze. Next, my own immunity system decided I obviously had no strength. Icing never does. My immunity decided it might as well eat away at my frosted muscles. My blood stopped circulating to my hands. "Hello body! I need my hands to hold on for what is next. I need my muscles to have the strength required of me. I need to circulate through my present circumstances." I felt consumed. I had to rein in what was going on in my reality.

I began to ask myself questions as I took inventory. "What the h*#% is going on? Why is my body failing me now? Raina, what are you thinking? Eating? Feeling?" I pressured myself for answers. My mind was chaotic, with thoughts going round and round. My emotions were unstable. My body surrendered to my own defenses – Anxiety. Mistrust. Apprehension. Uncertainty. Sadness – all umbrellaed under vehement fear, wide open to the elements of my personal Armageddon.

I knew I had to do something fast or I wouldn't have the strength to endure. I went back to questioning myself. I began with, "Who are You, and what are you going to do about this?"

"Who am I, you dare ask me?" I replied from somewhere deep inside, "I am a MOTHER!" I am pretty sure fire shot out of my own eyes while streaming through my muscular structure, melting the icing that had rendered me motionless at times. I was copping a 'tude with myself. "I am a grandmother, and a daughter to a woman who needs me now more than ever. I am a sister. A wife. And a damn good friend, if I must say so myself."

My intellectual posture was reviving. And I knew my emotions would come into alignment. I made all the necessary dietary and psychological changes to enable my body's renewal, just like Josiah was in the process of doing. We were in this together.

Mom's Strength, Mom's Wisdom

It was not until Josiah was diagnosed that I truly understood what my mother must have gone through. How she hid her tears and continued.

When I was thirteen, my twenty-eight-year-old sister Joann became extremely ill. Her immune system ceased to function properly. In the 1970s, doctors were still baffled by autoimmune issues, and Lupus was a complete mystery. There were none of the medicines we have today. Over a two-year period, Joanne's body slowly withdrew its strength from her. My parents would be faced with the unimaginable task of burying their oldest child, who, in fact, had been their only child for the first thirteen years of her life.

How my mother must have ached to be with her!

How she must have just wanted to crawl into bed and let the days pass through, with each breath, longing for Joann. Yet she rose. In truth, I do not remember her tears, or much of her story, as back then talking about such issues was taboo. At 15 years old, I was left to figure out my sibling grief on my own. Mom and Dad had checked out and I didn't even know it. They were not going to show it. Especially my mom. She never said anything, but my sense is she was going to show me, and the world, that she was strong.

My mom had a unique way of knowing. She would listen to her friends' situations and give them the precise wisdom they needed. She was their wise council. Not mine, though, oh heck no. My mother would give me the best of the best wisdom and I would reject it. How could she possibly know what I needed to do? Then a friend would say the same advice and I would jump on it. "Wow, thanks, that makes total sense!" Yes, I recognized my mother had said the same thing, but her words were on the reject list in my brain. I would shelf her info. My own need for independent thought now helped me understand Josiah's need to determine his own path. Afterall, I had cultivated it.

It had taken me a while before I finally thought, "Hmm, maybe Mom isn't so wrong after all. Maybe, just maybe, I want to pay attention to her thoughts." I knew Josiah was shelving all my wisdom too. I understood the ebb and flow of needing to work things out on my own and the guidance of my parents. My mom wanted to step in and help me with everything, but she couldn't, and neither could I for my son.

My mother, I learned, was able to keep her heart

from completely unraveling because she had been communicating with my sister all along. She would talk with Joann, inquire of her thoughts about things going on in her life. She also talked *about* my sister. A lot. In a saintly way. Which is understandable.

My brother Eddie, just two years my senior, was a career addict. It pains me to write that, but it is true. He started way too young, when the cool way to get high was sniffing paint or gasoline. He never thought those innocent junior high school capers would lock him in to a life inescapable.

He and my mother were conjoined because of his affliction. She loved him unconditionally. She saw his pain and his issues as an illness. She held him up – partly so he wouldn't fall, but mostly so she could remain standing.

It wasn't until Josiah was facing cancer that I understood how affliction conjoins a mother and her child even more than usual.

Joann was thirty years old when she transitioned to Spirit. I was fifteen. Thirty years later, when Eddie was forty-seven and I was forty-five, my mother would once again have to process the grief of her only son – the one, she maintained, had never crossed her – transitioning back to source.

This time, I do remember her tears. I do remember her heartache. I had been watching her pain in their adult relationship for all those years. She was devastated while he was here, and even more devastated when he left. She blamed herself for not doing more. Yet deep within, she knew he was sick.

She would come to terms with this quickly on the outside once more. She would rise again. Her strength was supernatural to me. She was working through it, communing with my father as well, who had crossed when I was thirty-three. Of course, she was! I would hear her talking to him. She would tell me how she was going to ask my dad about something, or say, "I asked your dad about this or that." It all made sense to me. My mom had connected to her husband and children in spirit. That is how she rose.

She saw the value in moving through and standing tall. My mother had me later in life, so she was in her eighties when my brother passed. She would often remind my younger sister Sheri and I that, "I have two daughters left!" My mother had learned to live in gratitude for what she did have.

She continued to be the wise woman for her friends. I still would push back a bit when she would forget I was in my fifties and give me her unsolicited advice. But no words of hers were ever shelfed again, only processed later, and with the understanding that she was always on point.

I never did tell my mom about Josiah's diagnosis. Sheri and I agreed that we did not need to add worry, unless there came a time she needed to know. She never did.

I wanted her support more than anything, when I was drowning in the fears that a cancer diagnosis instills in a mother. I wanted her to wrap her arms around me and dry my tears and tell me she would take care of everything. But more than that, I wanted to protect her fragile heart and mind.

At ninety-four years young, my mother's life began to wind down. She was getting tired. Six months before she crossed through the translucent door, she announced she had a new boyfriend, Paul. They were like teenagers. They no longer wanted to go hang out and play games in the rec room, they were happy just to be together, alone, watching TV and chatting. The caregivers were so concerned. They wanted them to be more active. But Mom was happy. Sheri and I watched them together and thought, how can we deny them this sacred moment in time? A boyfriend in her nineties? How fortunate was she!

Paul had an eye for my mother from the moment he arrived at the independent living home, and she did for him. I watched in awe. My mom needed brief moments of support when she was alone, and Paul was there. It gave us comfort. One night my mom was having a particularly hard evening. I was called to come, and when I got there Paul had taken care of her, like a lifelong husband would. I was shocked by the way he knew her and knew exactly what to do.

I lost my breath, and nearly my consciousness, when my father showed me it was him. He was there, orchestrating this.

I called my sister and shared my new insight, "Sheri, I think Paul might have died, and dad took over his body so he could come take care of Mom!" I know this is farfetched, but I am not kidding; their relationship was uncanny. It was as if my dad was dwelling inside Paul's body, and Mom could feel it. She loved Paul and just wanted to be with him.

Before my mother passed, Sheri and I took Mom shoe shopping, then to lunch. As we waited for our food, I asked her to tell me about Sheri. She would usually go into a story about when Sheri was a little girl, but this time she turned to Sheri and spoke of the present. She talked about Sheri's work, and how much she is loved by her friends, and who she was as a daughter. Mom's baby.

Amazed and awed, I turned to Sheri. "Sheri, she spoke of exactly who you are right now!" Sheri quivered in astonishment, "Mom, tell Sheri about me!"

Mom laid her hand out across the table for me to take. I took it, and she looked me in the eyes and said:

"You... well, you are gifted, and you know you're gifted!"

As she spoke, I could feel her wisdom and the hundreds of grandmothers before her stream down her arm, through her hand, to mine, and up into my soul. I began to weep uncontrollably. My sister stared silent. This was the deepest, most beautiful gift my mother had ever given me. My heart, soul and spirit opened and all the words this woman ever spoke to me poured off the shelves, flooding this daughter's heart. Her impact on my life revealed in one sentence, that, is now carrying me through the rest of my time on earth.

My mom left this planet two months later. Paul was moved out of the independent living home within the next couple of months. My dad had her now. Paul's mission had been completed.

Dr. U

The "C" word disrupts an entire village, not just the person whose body is poked, prodded, and judged by pirates dressed in doctor's clothing.

I am not saying all doctors are pirates. By no means. I was raised by one. I hold most doctors in extremely high esteem. However, there are the few, like Dr. X, who do not take the time to sit with their patients, calm their fears, and encourage them to follow the trail that leads them to wellness.

Our encounter with Dr. X had left Josiah with such an uncomfortable feeling towards Western medicine. I encouraged him to seek out another doctor. Hesitantly, he agreed.

We found an amazing, understanding doctor at Orange County Children's Hospital; we will call him "Dr. U." for understanding. I have no memory of what led us here, but I suppose it was someone's recommendation. Josiah liked Dr. U very much, and when he told him he wanted to give a holistic approach a chance, Dr. U agreed that was possible. Dr. U still wanted to treat him with chemo, but said his approach would be different from that of Dr. X. He would treat Josiah the way he would treat a teenager, meaning the dosing would be less intensive. When Josiah said he wanted to do it his way first, Dr. U said okay, he would watch over him for a short season. This felt like a miracle to us. I guess the doctor forgot to inform his nurse, because she would call Josiah daily, "encouraging" him (and I use the term loosely) to get scheduled for chemotherapy. Josiah would beg her to stop, but she was insistent. We went back to see Dr. U, who now agreed with his nurse while concurrently agreeing with Josiah. He again told Josiah that he may be able to use a natural approach to heal... he just could not do it with him because he was bound by the rules of the hospital. We left Dr. U's office both encouraged and discouraged. We had thought we had found our perfect guide, now we had to step up the quest on our own. We both knew there had to be a protocol that would clear this beast and allow my son to get back to college, and his life.

The Quest

Here is the thing. The quest for healing has many vines. Josiah, being the monkey he is, was going to climb every one of them.

My bohemian son. NO diagnosis was going to set him back; instead, it catapulted him.

He did finish his third year of college as he began his healing journey. He changed his diet radically. Became a raw foodist. So much so, he was hired at a raw food restaurant and became quite the cook.

We found a local naturopathic doctor and began vitamin-infused treatments. He had a daily protocol and was strict with himself.

On the outside he looked the same. But internally he was changing. My now twenty-one-year-old son was emerging. Evolving. His external appearance would soon follow.

Josiah was transforming from the now Orange

County college yuppy into a full blown, down to the core of the earth, deep and introspective hippie.

By the end of his third year of college, what he was, and who he was, were dancing with who he was becoming.

That is when I got the call.

"Mom?" Why is there a questioning in his voice, I thought? "I have been thinking..." Oh dear, Josiah is cut from my cloth, for sure. If he is thinking, and there is questioning in his voice, he is full of ideas and I am in for a long conversation.

"I think I want to be a massage therapist!"

"Okay, that's awesome! We can open a day spa/herb shop one day!" I had always been onboard for a collective with my kids.

"I mean, I do not want to go back for my fourth year of college. I want to do it now!"

"Say what?!" I stammered. "Josiah, you have one more year. Just finish and then go to massage school!" Even as I said the words, I knew they would land on deaf ears. His mind was made up. It was going to take an act of Divine intervention to change it, not a mother's petitioning pleas.

He was determined that this was the next road. As much as I wanted him to finish with his degree in theater design, I wanted him to walk his own journey more. There was no need to argue my point (not that I did not repeat myself several times). When life hands you a diagnosis like the one it handed Josiah, well, let's just say, I could not stand in the way of his evolution.

The Cyr Wheel

Josiah continued to work at Disney all through college. He had met so many interesting friends, and he loved every one of them for their uniqueness. Two of these "uniquenicks" were Nicholas and Nick. They were acrobatic and funny. They introduced him to Sam Tribble, who owned a nearby gym. Sam and Josiah became fast friends, and Josiah would go to the gym to practice his art and play on the equipment. Sam lived in Corona del Mar at the time and would spin the Cyr wheel above China Cove, inviting anyone who wanted to join in. The Cyr wheel (also known as the monowheel, or simple wheel) is an acrobatic apparatus that consists of a single large ring made of aluminum or steel with a diameter approximately ten to fifteen centimeters (four to six inches) taller than the performer. The performer stands inside the Cyr wheel and grasps its rim, causing it to roll and spin like a penny while performing acrobatic moves in and around the rotating wheel.

Josiah, who was a sponge for anything acrobatic, immediately fell in love with the Cyr wheel. Soon, he was going to Sam's house to help him assemble Cyr wheels and learn more about the process.

Later, Josiah would help Sam build their first portable 24' x 24' floor for spinning. Once Josiah was interested in something, there was no half-assing it. He was in all the way. He took the wheel everywhere – down by the beach, in malls, and of course on stage, where he would spin his way right into the hearts of the audience.

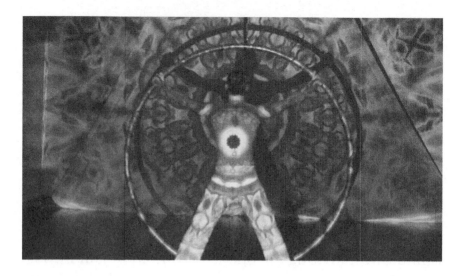

Isabella

Massage school proved to be the perfect path for the transformation that was occurring simultaneously within him. His school of choice opened a world that he was familiar with but had not really dabbled in until that point. He began to study everything – not just about massage but spiritual evolution. What was going on in the ethers. Time. Purpose. Soul journey. Shamanism. Angels. Meditation. Energy. You name it, he was checking it out, which made for some amazing conversations between us.

One day, at a spirit fair down in Orange County, Josiah found himself drawn to Isabella, a strikingly beautiful tall woman with wavy blond hair, who was enthralling the crowd with her shamanistic expression. When she was done speaking, he walked over to her and said, "I think you can help me."

Isabella could clearly see the swollen lymph on his neck. "Yes, I can!"

She began to work on him. Running energy through him. Using her shaman magic to help reduce the swelling. When she was done, they both stood in the brilliance of the energy that surrounded them. They gazed upon his lymph that had shrunk right before their eyes.

Their friendship was solidified in that moment. Josiah followed her home, which would soon become a refuge for him. Through Isabella, he was introduced to a tribe of like-minded friends seeking similar ways of life and healing. He would hang out at her home while she had fire ceremonies and trade his massage techniques for her shaman magic. Right before her eyes, he was growing. Her student was becoming her teacher as well.

One day, he was at Isabella's when a powerful knowing came to him.

"Isabella!" he exclaimed, making sure he had her full attention, "I met you for my mom!"

I am pretty sure that he called me within minutes of making that statement. "Mom, you need to meet Isabella!" He was adamant about it.

Here he was – gleaning so much friendship, healing, and expansion with her and her tribe. Yet he knew a grander reason for his encounter with her. Me... Me? He was always thinking of me. Isabella was the first, but certainly not the last friend he met on his spiritual quest, who he insisted I meet too.

Josiah left his indelible mark on Isabella as well, just as he did with everyone in his life. To this day, way up in the giant tree of her meditative backyard, where monkeys fly, or should I say Josiah, is the hammock he tied there over ten years ago.

John the Flute Maker

Josiah finished massage school and graduated as a Holistic Health Practitioner. He felt confident in his journey. Isabella remained close. She was traveling out to Joshua Tree and felt Josiah needed to meet John, fondly named "John the Flute maker."

John and Josiah had an immediate connection, as if they had always known each other. John's gift of making and playing the flute mesmerized Josiah, who'd had a thing for the flute since junior high. It was not a question of if Josiah would play one of John's flutes, only when. And, as it turned out, it was right then. It was as if his natural ability to play now lived within him. It was kismet.

The day I met John, a few short months after that, I had the same realization. I was not graced with a new ability to play the flute, but I was given a brother and a knowing that John and Josiah were bonded, and he would guide Josiah as a spiritual father.

Boulder Gardens

After the visit with John, Isabella took Josiah out to Boulder Gardens, which is six-hundred forty acres of huge majestic boulders and vistas. (Remember Nancy and her message I dismissed? This was where he was headed.)

Isabella, who had experienced the power of this sacred land, knew Josiah would benefit from being there. Little did she realize he would want to stay...and by stay, I mean move there. This land had seen holy people, lightworkers, monks, and seekers of higher dimensions. They were drawn there to meditate, reflect, create, and revive. Josiah could feel it and needed to cocreate in this energy. Garth, the owner of Boulder Gardens, welcomed Josiah. He gave him free range to create. Josiah was blown away when he realized there was an unfinished project on top of one of the boulders. Josiah enlisted his dad, Jeremy, and his "Halfling" (half-brother) Michael, along with several of his friends, to help him create his next dwelling: a magical dome home on top of that boulder. He worked the land as he continued to study holistic medicine and Spirit. He wrote. He painted. He was becoming acquainted with his new persona.

He met the local performers and continued to perform his circus antics.

I watched him shapeshifting, like a transformer.

Fortunately, Pioneer town is only one hour from me. When Josiah tired of the heat, or just needed his time with me, he would come home. Sometimes for a few days or sometimes a few weeks. Though he no longer sucked his thumb with my hair wrapped around it, we continued to speak in our secret gibberish language. I was grateful for those precious moments when he needed to connect with me, just as he had when he was a little boy.

Binah & Elijah

During this time, Josiah met many travelers and passersby, who would come and stay on the land.

Artists. Performers. Sages. Seekers of the higher realms. Josiah gleaned their wisdom, eager to understand their pilgrimage. Then there were the soul connections. The ones he would join with, traveling to festivals, performing and captivating the audiences with his juggling, acrobatics, spinning and humor. In between, he would help his artistic friends sell their specialty items and give treatments to whoever needed his healing touch.

My vagabond and poet was also becoming a sage.

Though Orange County would call him back to her, he was still drawn to the desert. For a season he went back and forth between Orange County, my house and Joshua Tree. He wanted the best of all worlds: the ocean, the desert and, thank goodness, his Mommaz home sweet home.

Circus, Disney, the Cyr wheel, massage school and all these mini-adventures were puzzle pieces that fit together and led him to a place like no other. A place that had a key. An emotional key. The gene keys. And a key to his heart that unlocked a Josiah even I had never seen.

One of these festivals was called Tribal Conversion, a wild, artistic, and spirit-filled festival that draws thousands of people from all over. Josiah was wandering, doing his own magic, when he came across a lovely artist creating a mural. She felt his vibe and turned to him. "My name is Binah," she said, "And this is Elijah, my fiancé. Will you join us?" Josiah immediately joined in. He could see her vision, and together they created her D.N.A. tree of life mural.

They were sure they had always known each other. She turned to Elijah, and asked, "Can we keep him?"

And keep him they did.

OneDoorLand

Josiah came back from this experience with yet another idea, and this time he was coming to tell me about it in person. Clearly it was going to be big.

He wanted to move to OneDoorLand. In Portland. Over a thousand miles away from me. No wonder he knew a phone call wasn't going to fly.

How can I tell a twenty-four-year-old man-child, "No, absolutely not! You cannot move that far from your mother?" The answer is, you can't tell him. You can listen to his reasoning. Understand his thoughts, and hope he will continue to keep you as close as he has up to now.

He packed up his worlds from Joshua Tree and what was left in Orange County, came home for the few weeks before setting off on this grand adventure.

I wrestled with my own version of what was happening. How would he stay well and keep the "C" at bay if he were so far away? Not that I had been his personal nurse. He was his own health advocate. That is what I had taught him to be. But, should the "what if" happen, I would not be able to close the thousand miles between us nearly as I could the fifty.

I muted these alarms in my head. They were useless. Living in the uncertainties was not going to serve either of us. Living in the what ifs of the yeses to his health and happiness was.

We loaded up what looked like a vintage moving truck. White with no words on it. I sucked up every emotion that would make him feel uncomfortable as he climbed into the driver's seat. His long brown hair, genuine smile, and deep brown eyes were powerfully expressing to me that he was the picture of the to-morrows he was heading for. "Don't worry, Mom. I will be fine."

I unloaded an abbreviated version of what I had muted, until he drove around the corner and was unable to detect the waterworks.

Remember my inner dialogue on the way to see the oncologist: "...and there will be flowers, and butterflies, and mystical creatures following him?" How I had seen his healing as I wanted it? Well, I had seen it! That was exactly the road he had chosen, and OneDoorLand only amplified it.

OneDoorLand is an alchemical artistic sanctuary. A small community of musicians, artists, and tea monks. This was the community Josiah had been looking for. A place where everyone felt like he did, about the earth, art, life, love, and the elements.

For Josiah, it was also like a shot of creative adrenaline. He started designing what I call "Wooden Wonders." His energetic field was expanding. He had just been reunited with another part of his soul family. He loved it up there. He was doing things he knew deep down he wanted to do but hadn't realized it until he began doing them.

He would call me almost daily, with a new idea that he, of course, wanted to teach me. But I was open. If I have learned anything from this whole mothering experience, it is that our children are our biggest teachers.

He would read me accounts of vivid dreams he was having. Send me pictures of unimaginable wooden craftsmanship. He was designing clothes and boots, building yurts, and creating art. He had a love of the elements, water, air, stonework, crystals and the power of healing with music. He began creating his own flute music. He would weave his music in during his healing treatments, use plant medicine, essential oils, his intuition and all the wisdom and alchemy he had learned over the years, to facilitate healing with his clients.

I was in love with him loving his new home. He was encapsulating everything he had learned and loved into an eclectic energy of healing. So unique and so alchemical that he was given the name:

Josiah, The Elf Alchemist.

Only one thing was missing. The Cyr Wheel. Josiah told Sam they should bring Spinnovation (Sam's Spin Classes) to Portland. Elijah agreed and created beautiful choreographed videos of Josiah spinning to music and color. They put together a campaign and birthed Cyr wheel classes for all ages.

But Portland had a downside. The cold winters tested Josiah's lungs continuously. He tried every concoction he could to find relief, but the wet climate was winning. He muscled through the winters because, along with everything else, Portland and OneDoorLand conjured up in his life.

I believe the purest reason he was there was this:

Love!

"Open up to love. Do not be afraid to cry, to love, to show emotion. Breathe in the love around you and allow your voice to sing. The truth of your love will shine unto the world and you will never be lonely again. Open up to love!"

~Josiah David

Rain

I never knew what to expect when my phone was ringing, and Josiah was the caller. His voice was considerably different on this call. I did not feel worried, though, just bewildered by his unfamiliar tone.

"Mom!!!" he exclaimed.

I immediately sat down on my bed. "Yes, what's going on?" I knew he had something to tell me that was beyond our already diverse topics of conversation.

"Mom! I met her!"

My eyes widened. Oh yes, this was something I had been waiting to hear. "Tell me more," I cried softly.

He giggled as he continued. "Her name is Rain!"

"Are you serious? Really? Rain?"

"Yes! Mom! Rain! She is the one. My soulmate."

This was big.

"Tell me everything!" I hummed out from the depth of my soul. "Wait, aren't you driving home from Seattle right now?"

"Yes" he answered, "that is where I met her!"

Josiah had been up in Seattle visiting his college friends. A group of them went out for a hike. Rain was among the group. They had an instant connection. Their conversations were soulful and inspiring. He was captivated.

"There is only one issue..." He paused. "She is seventeen. She'll be eighteen in a few months, though?" His tone grew questioning at the end, as if he thought I would disapprove.

"Oh yes, that *is* young!" I said. I could tell he had his own apprehensions, but only about the age difference (he was then twenty-five). He went on to describe how he felt. What was going on within him. And within her.

"Oh Josiah, that is no soulmate, she is your twin flame," I blurted. What he was experiencing fancied something all too familiar to me. "It feels similar, I know, but soulmates connect over lifetimes and can be romantic or not. Twin flames are different and more intense. From my understanding, you only have one twin flame, which makes perfect sense, if they are the other half of your soul and not just part of your soul family. You are usually so much alike, like you are describing. It is amazing and difficult, but it is doable!"

"As soon as I met her and we locked eyes," he said, "I knew!"

About six months prior, Josiah had been in deep meditation. During that meditative state he heard a voice calling the name, "Akoya," and realized the voice was calling out to him. When he acknowledged the voice, a female energetic figure appeared with long blond hair. Josiah sensed Akoya was another part of him, his spirit/artist side, and began using the name Josiah Akoya –changing it on social media and signing his wooden wonders and art with it, and walking in what he felt was a deeper connection to his soul's journey. When Josiah locked eyes with Rain, the woman in his vision was who he saw. He knew in that moment that Akoya also had something to do with Rain, that they had been together before.

"That is exactly how it felt, Mom, I feel like she is me!" The words blew out of his mouth in an exhale.

Drawn together in the winds of change; Love re-defined in a single moment. I witnessed his heart expanding into something he had never perceived. True, untouched imagining; that love was real. And possibly endless.

They were two peas in the same pod. You think that might have thrown me for a loop. Would he stop speaking his babble to me, would our secret language now be foreign? Not a chance. He was bigger than that. He contained multiple secret languages. And could share them with everyone he loved.

But the energetic language he and Rain shared was cosmic. A love you want to wrap yourself inside of and share with them. Living poetry. She was he, and I could feel it. The female version of Josiah. The muse and the magician weaving through the ethers of energetic connection. It was beautiful to be the witness of their love, that they sprinkled on all of us. The missing link of his being. Manifested in Rain.

Their adventure began in Portland, but these two like-minded forest elves were going to wander down the coast and through the mountains of California to me. Josiah was not just bringing her for an introduction. He was showing me how connected they truly were.

Now let me tell you. Telling your mom you are going to travel down the coast, and be in the forest without cell service? And while she has concerns about your health? It was a tricky quest he set me on once more.

Yet his own quest, for life within his diagnosis, had everyone marveling at him. Was he in denial? Or, was he going to make the most of what the earth realm had to offer, no matter what was in store for him, unwilling to allow it to define him?

Oh, anticipation is a cruel emotion when your baby is coming to see you. Excuse me, *youngest child.* He forbade me to call him my baby after he met Rain. But I still did, always correcting myself with "youngest child" afterwards.

He checked in with me when cell service was available, but those couple of weeks still felt like a year. And yes, I am that crazy mother, and grandmother, who runs outside with tears flowing down my face when my children arrive.

And, just like Josiah, from the minute my eyes met Rain's, I knew her too. I understood everything he had been telling me. Like *clarity* had her own voice. Staying with me for days, or months, felt natural to Rain, and to me. She was the extension of Josiah. Part of him, and now part of me.

Travels and the Zoo Life

Josiah had always kept in touch with his YMCA circus trainer, Pete. Pete had expanded over the years – traveling the world; choreographing circus entertainment. One of his venues was the San Diego Zoo, and he enlisted Josiah's talent, on more than one occasion. Josiah was grateful for the gig and the reprieve from the Portland weather.

This time he would be performing all summer in their outback skit. Josiah was the Tasmanian devil – kind of befitting since he was here, and then there, and then here. He would slide down the cables over the audience, climb down a pole and jump into his Cyr wheel, spinning in true Taz fashion. All the while, creating facial expressions that bewitched and charmed the audience.

When he was performing, all inhibitions, fears, and self-doubts would leave him. He would step into his character and become it.

When the summer ended, Rain and Josiah came back to my home. They stayed for a bit and then it was back up to Portland. He would travel back and forth, repeating his zoo performances for several years until an opportunity to live in Kauai presented itself.

Just writing these words, (moving to Kauai) my eyes roll back and the weight of them makes my head fall backwards. Truth be told, by this time I had settled into his bohemian ways.

Rain and her dad had made plans to travel long before Josiah entered the scene. And this trip was coming up upon them swiftly.

Pete had hired Josiah to do a Christmas gig at the zoo, this time as one of Santa's elves. Also befitting. He packed up Portland once more and headed home, bags and boxes in tow. Oh, how this would have delighted me, if only my garage was going to be more than a pitstop on the way to Hawaii.

Rain and Josiah stayed with me for over six weeks this time. Josiah's holiday visits were not always on the actual holiday, which never really bothered me. But this year he was home for Christmas. He decorated the tree and cooked a vegan lasagna to add his touch to our family meal. We all had to take pause at how amazing his food was. He had become quite the cook. This was a special Christmas. One that is sealed in my heart differently than the others.

After the holidays, Rain set off to meet up with her

father. Josiah prepared to move to Kauai. The plan was for Josiah to set up house there; then, when Rain's adventure with her dad was done, she would meet him, and they would continue their journey together.

I had to give this adventure up to the Universe.

Josiah did set up house and Rain joined him, but way earlier than planned, the adventure with her dad thwarted by her uncompromising need to be with her other half.

Living poetry defines reason.

Disappointed, Kevin, Rain's father, forfeited. He threw up the white flag and surrendered to their magic that was outside of any of our control. Including theirs.

For these true nomads, Kauai turned out to be a short endeavor. I think it always was going to be. Maybe that is why I could let this one go to the Universe, and not my vessel that had held every move he had made. Together they flew back home and stayed with me until they headed back down to San Diego for yet another gig at the zoo. After the summer, they both met me in Utah for a week of learning about health, healing, and essential oils. A rare treat for this momma for sure.

In the days that followed, I could tell that they were going in and out of being fully present at the conference, and with me. Not that unusual for young lovers, but this was different. Strange. The week was busy with classes and people. Josiah and Rain were in two separate cars and I could feel an imbalance and disconnect around them. It made me feel off-centered. Then the conference was over, and my traveling companions were in their cars waiting. Except Rain and Josiah. I told my carload

I would be right back. I was going to go say goodbye to them, again.

I walked up to the rental home that had just housed us with such enthusiasm. I opened the door to what felt like an empty container that had no voice. They were thick in conversation, and I was, without question, going to interrupt.

"What's going on?" I questioned, the tears already forming and peaking over the rim of my eyes. "What? What? What's happening?" I asked again. Neither of them wanted to say a word. They knew if they did the reality of what they were speaking before I entered the house would come true. Their eyes looked like mine, rimmed with fluid that was creeping its way forward.

Josiah spoke first. "Rain is going to Nevada City and I am going to Portland." I understood but kept myself in denial as long as I could. I wanted to speak, tell them no, but he continued. "We are taking a break."

This idea had been tossed around for a while now but never manifested. They loved each other, there was no question about that. But Rain was young, and felt she needed to experience a little more of life before she settled down with Josiah. Josiah was ready. He had no doubt and no need to experience any part of the rest of his life without her. But he understood, for, after all, they were the same. He had been a nomad. He understood the need and the struggle her heart and soul were in. He was not going to hold her back. He was going to hold her up.

Here he was. Holding the love of his life in his arms as their hearts broke, telling her it was okay, he understood. This girl who had completed him was going in a different direction. What would he do without her? I held them both as we all wept, tears streaming unchecked down our faces.

My ride was honking. We had a twelve-hour drive home and they needed coffee. The three of us exited the silent house that now contained our brokenhearted tears. Each one of us got into the cars that would take us in different directions. My carload went to the first coffee shop we could find. I ordered a green matcha. The rain was falling in sync with the tears I was secreting. I was so in love with their love, I just couldn't wrap my head around it. My stomach ached and my speech was slowing down.

"Raina! You are white as a ghost!" Elicia, my friend and the driver, exclaimed.

"Pull over!" I told her.

"It's pouring," she stated the obvious as she stopped the car. I opened the door. Not a sprinkle was coming down on me, or the car. I darted out about fifteen steps, and then, green matcha hit the ground. I took a deep breath, ran back to the car, shut the door and instantly it began to pour rain again. I pulled out my phone and called Josiah to make sure he was not on the side of the road in anguish also. He wasn't. He had had more time to process it.

I, on the other hand, would never drink green matcha again.

Endless Rain

He was doing alright in Portland. Massage, stonework, and sound healing with his flute. He was creating wooden wonders that had a voice of their own, and he was teaching and performing with his Cyr wheel. He was in his full Elf Alchemist persona and feeling like he would survive after Rain.

One reason was apparent. Rain and Josiah would never lose contact. She and he worked hard to find their way to themselves, while maintaining their deep connection and friendship. Rain looked to Josiah for his magical wisdom that came from a place no one other could reach. Rain gave him hope. Hope in everything eternal.

As much as it pained him to parallel this way, he came to a place where he could lay the pain to the side. He loved her completely.

Dr. W.W.

Months went by before he came down for another visit. We all gathered at Jeremy's house for dinner and play. Josiah looked good, but thin.

I was concerned about his lack of a qualified holistic doctor. He had found holistic healers at every junction and had encountered so many wise healers – each one teaching him, and showing him, the possibilities that each protocol had to offer. We had been to him. And her. And done this. And that. But since he had been back in Portland, we had not found anyone. And I sensed evidence in his body.

I pulled Mitchell aside. I told him what was racing through my head. He agreed. This was a priority.

I began my own search for such practitioners in Portland. I told Josiah about the doctors I had found, and he agreed to check them out. He went in to interview the first doctor and was immediately impressed with what this facility had to offer. We will call this doctor Dr. W.W., for "went wrong." Dr. WW was amazing. He took into account everything Josiah had been through. He was impressed and concerned at the same time. And he was exceptional at communicating with me. My rule from the beginning was that I could talk to every doctor. Josiah always obliged.

The Portland winter was on its way once more. This year, Josiah's body would have an extreme reaction to it. Adding to this reaction, was the protocol Dr. WW had put him on.

Thanksgiving 2015

This Thanksgiving, Richard and I, along with Jeremy and his family, traveled through the snowy roads to Southern Oregon. Josiah was in Portland, which is in the northern part of the state, just a five-hour drive away rather than the usual seventeen hours to my house. He was elated that we would be so close and made the trip to join us. He arrived a day after we did, and as I ran out to greet him, I could tell that Portland's winter sky had opposed Josiah much more cruelly than in years past. This chilled me colder than the snow that was falling and blanketing the earth beside me.

We talked at length. I wanted him to move home. Nothing new about that. I asked again, knowing this would be his gracious reply: "No. You know that is not going to happen, Mom!" We agreed on one thing, though. It was time for a protocol change.

I twisted Richard's ear on our drive back to California. Tormented with fear. I repeated myself over and over, replaying the scene and conversations Josiah and I had shared. When I got home, I contacted one of our local naturopaths who is an associate of mine. I wanted her thoughts. She suggested NAET.

NAET is a blending of the non-invasive procedures from Western and Eastern healing practices. It helps to eliminate allergies of all kinds, permanently. It is a specific treatment procedure formulated by combining chiropractic and Chinese Medicine principles applied through spinal manipulation, acupuncture, kinesiology, acupressure and nutrition specific to your issues, body, and constitution.

She believed Josiah's body was rejecting the treatments Dr. WW had prescribed because his immune system was compromised, creating an allergic reaction to nearly everything. I described this to Josiah. He chatted with her as well and came to the same conclusion. NAET was exactly what he felt he needed.

He quickly found a practitioner in Portland. Within a few weeks he began to feel better. The treatments were helping him not only physically, but mentally as well. He had a restored conviction in his direction, and his practice.

He was determined to push through. He would continue to perform, do his breathing treatment and call me for words of adoration. Then back on stage he would go, the audience clueless to his travails.

But the Portland weather was one allergy that refused to fade away.

Santa Cruz

Josiah had wanted to live in Santa Cruz since the day he had met Jesse and Margot in Joshua Tree, seven and a half years earlier, at the start of this soul journey of healing. Jesse and Margot were among those he'd traveled to festivals with and helped sell their beautiful yogi and elven clothing. They too had wanted him to come live where they lived, on a beautiful piece of property in the hills of Santa Cruz. But there had not been space for him.

They talked often and now more than ever he hoped there was space. He shared with them one more time of his plight. The Portland winters. This time, this phone call would bring good news. Margot told him a place would soon be opening.

Josiah packed up his Portland world once more and headed to their property to wait for his space. But waiting proved too much for him. He was still the outdoorsman of yesteryears, but sleeping outdoors or in his vehicle was no longer the adventure it used to be. He needed a bed and the warmth of home. I needed that for him as well. His search for a room to rent didn't take him long. The choice being the first multi-living Victorian home that he found in town. Of course, in just one meeting the tenants were smitten by him, and he, them. And just like that, he had found a space to call home.

His room was a ten by twelve dwelling with twelve-foot ceilings. Not enough space. He decided building a wooden loft that he could put his mattress on would be his first task. He nested his dresser and computer desk beneath the loft and still had enough room for a smaller mattress he would call his couch. Several of the roommates fell in love with the loft idea and commissioned him to help them make one for their rooms as well. He was already having an impact on the strangers he would soon call family.

Santa Cruz had the perfect energy. The ocean and the mountains at his fingertips. A plethora of health food stores and vegan restaurants. He found his salt float friends. Coffee shops with local art hanging from their walls, where he knew could hang his art as well.

The streets were woven with everything he had envisioned. People and places that reflected Josiah. Despite the traffic, he felt he had found a utopia of sorts. He had ideas and was going to make them happen.

But his body was inconsistent with him. Determined to steady it, he joined the local gym. He knew if he could use his body in the way it was used to, it would align, and he would move through the temporary slowdown he was experiencing.

He would restructure his diet and create art.

He hung out, singing and playing with his multitalented housemates. He enjoyed the fresh air of inventiveness and was witnessing himself within this new existence he had created.

Still, his body continued to fluctuate. Phone calls would pour in. One. Two. Sometimes three a day. He was so frustrated. So over not being able to breathe because of the congestion that had plagued him off and on his entire life.

And most of all, over the monster that loomed within his body, reminding him to stay solid in his convictions about healing.

His truth was he was healed. And he walked in that truth.

His first year in Santa Cruz went smooth. But Northern California can be cold, and the warmer weather of this seaside city was taking its sweet time in 2017.

Oh My Heart

(I wrote this one morning in the summer of 2017 as he slept, and I lamented over his health.)

Oh, my heart my sorrow

Oh, my heart my soul

Oh, my creator please hear me

Oh, my hands feel cold

Beneath this layer of longing

Between the outstretched miles

Behind My whispers, behind my smile

I need you

I don't want to give it a voice

I intend to keep my speech slow

I breathe in a rhythm with his

Touch His life his soul

Touch the parts unnerving

Touch what no one beholds

Touch me, touch him

All I have are these wishes

All I want is him whole

All is all in your answer

Answer me swift, Answer me yes

Oh, my heart, Oh my soul

It Speaks Louder Than I Can Hear

Josiah was complaining of an odd rash. He said it was traveling around his body. But he never sent pictures. He had already planned a trip to visit us and knew his dad or I would certainly have remedies once he arrived.

He flew to his father's first. Mitchell was taken back at how the rash had taken over him. He was swelling and uncomfortable, the inflammation not allowing his skin to breathe.

This time it was Mitchell in full alarm. He sent me pictures, followed by an immediate phone call. His voice was rickety, and in his speech was a calm uneasiness. We may not be married anymore, but he still knows the tone to use when deep concern is involved so I don't fall to fragments. He was going to make an appointment to take Josiah to his Naturopath in the morning. The Naturopath did blood work and put him on a strict protocol.

Two days later, Michael, Josiah's halfling, drove him to me. I ran outside as soon as I saw Michael's blue truck pull into the driveway. Mitchell's calm speech had been unable to harness my fragmented woes. Josiah stepped out of the truck and I lost my footing. There was no way he could catch me, so I regained my composure as quickly as I lost it. I hugged him but even that was too much for his quarrelsome body.

I had just moved to this home two months prior, and he had not yet seen it. He had been anxiously wanting to be here, the place he too would call home. But the couch would be as far as we initially got. And that was okay. I had my Doctor Mommy hat on and nothing else mattered but getting him well.

Jeremy and Valerie were on their way. Along with the beekeeper who was going to harness the fifty thousand bees that had made a home in the barn on our property.

Valerie arrived first. Startled to tears that she shelved, in order to take care of her younger brother.

Jeremy arrived swiftly after. He talked with Josiah, made sure he was comfortable and headed to the bees to divert himself.

Josiah thought he was coming for a five-day visit. Needless to say, I asked him again to please move home, which we all knew was out of the question for Josiah. Mitchell approached him differently. "How about you stay down here with us until you are better? You can live between your mother's house and my house. Right now, you should be here with your family who loves you." Josiah agreed. Temporarily living with us was fine. Well played, Mitchell.

I could not see anything temporarily if I tried.

Healing Retreat

The summer of 2017 was the last one I would physically spend with my son. Finally, this child of mine, who had lived far from me for ten years, was going to spend the summer in Southern California. He would take in the love and hospitality of his father down near the beach, and mine, closer to the mountains.

He would deem this time in his journey his *Healing Retreat*.

My bohemian healer, in need of healing for his body that was wearying. It was an emotionally brutal and beautiful time. In the nine years we had spent keeping the monster at bay, his vitality had never been so challenged.

The brazen audacity of this damn dis-ease to infiltrate his body! He was suffering. And I was powerless. I wanted to sacrifice my life for his. My beautiful son. I could barely leave his side. I would cry whenever he traveled back to his father's. I pleaded and begged and bargained with the Ethereal, reminding him of his entrance. Sleep was minimal, as I listened with one ear through the night, like a mother with her newborn baby. Awakened at the sounds of him unsettled through the night. Creeping through the hallway, just to hear him breathing as he slept. And if he were awake, I would lie with him until his body settled. Most evenings, he would text me. "You awake?" And even if I wasn't, I was now, and would sleep with him until his dreams arrived.

I knew I had stepped into panic when, one morning, I saw that he was not up yet. I did not want to wake him if he was finally in a comfortable slumber. So, I opened the back door as quietly as I could, tiptoed to the window of his room, and looked in. I needed to know he was alright.

I was wrestling to stay in Josiah's version of me. The strong pillar of knowing what he needed.

Several weeks in, his mind and body were responding to our plea for healing. He began to feel better. Symptoms were withdrawing. His faith in alternative methods to combat illness were uncanny.

The Interview

In the midst of the intensity of this physical invasion, he was asked to come in for an interview at Apple, Inc., San Jose. The job: to be an onsite massage therapist.

"This is the job." he told me, "a massage therapist's dream job."

My mommy senses did not want him to fly up there. He was just entering the state of recovery.

Don't go. Stay with me. I thought, but never said. I knew my son. He was going.

I have always known and relentlessly told Josiah that he was magic. A guru. But he had never proven more magical, with all his talents, than he did at this interview.

They did not see his frailty from his summer illness; they did not see that his strength had been braved, and they did not see a man who had just been through the most excruciating, physical interruption of his life.

All they saw was his light. His wisdom. His humor. His radiance. And, his magic.

I had been in a meeting and missed two calls. While I was staring at the phone, praying that he was okay. He rang again.

"Hi baby, sorry I was in a meeting, what's up? You okay?"

"*Mom!* "I got the job!"

"Oh my gosh, Josiah!" I shrieked, "Are you serious? I told you, you are magic!"

I am Going with You

And with that, his Healing Retreat was coming to an end.

Apple wanted him to start in the next couple of weeks, and now he was eager to go home. Back to Santa Cruz.

Going on this interview was one thing, but completely abandoning the retreat and going home was another.

My need to take care of him was not over. I had to have a quick inner dialogue with myself. *This isn't your decision, Raina. It is the job he has always wanted. He is going. Make peace with it.* Then it hit me. *He has his bliss back.* I knew arguing was not an option.

He was down at his dad's when he called me to tell me his plans. "I am going to gather up my stuff then drive to your house tomorrow to get the rest. Give you a day, and head home."

My heart sank at the thought of him driving eight hours by himself after these tortuous months. I quickly processed his intentions and immediately thought: there is one last thing I can do for him, to bridge his healing retreat with his next chapter. Within seconds I called him back.

"Mom? What's up?"

"I'm going with you." I announced.

"Really?" he said, and I could feel his relief.

"Yes, I will stay with you for a couple of days. Help you get settled and then take the train home.

"Awesome!" flowed with multiple meanings of love and gratitude. I could feel it through the phone.

I am so grateful I listened to that inner knowing and traveled home with him. I was able to *mommy* him the entire time. Helping him reorganize his room, and space in the kitchen.

His roommates were so welcoming, as I invaded their home.

Going into Josiah's world, wherever he lived, had always been part of what we did. He would take me to all of his favorite places; stores, restaurants, hiking trails and of course, to see his friends. Santa Cruz was no different. He took me everywhere. We shopped his favorite natural food stores and ate at Dharma's vegan restaurant, several times. We hiked and floated in a saltwater float tank, a zero-gravity healing therapy. A long-awaited treat he had wanted to gift me. We listened to Lyndsey Sterling, the last artist he would turn me on to.

Had I been lazy or gave in to my tired soul, I would have missed this sacred moment in time, when all the chaos was calm, and the only thing that mattered was taking in the sights of our travels together, eating food, and listening to music.

"Either you allow it, or you prevent it."

~ Josiah "Akoya" David

The Train Station

I did not want to leave him, but my time in this role was over. He was ready to reenter his life.

We traveled through the mountains from Santa Cruz to the San Jose train station.

Little did I know that *these* mountains would soon betray me. And take him away.

He pulled up to the train station. He was excited to go straight to Apple after he dropped me off.

We took what would be our last picture together.

He handed me a four-foot strand of beads. "I want you to have these. They were made by a Buddhist nun." I looked at him, puzzled. "A Buddhist nun?" He smiled and wrapped the beads around my neck.

I began to act like a mother whose child was off to their first day of kindergarten. Attempting to take pictures of him getting ready to drive off in his truck.

"Mom!" his voice ever so slightly elevated. "Stop!" He hated when I made a fuss.

"Fine," I said, rolling my eyes. "I know."

I walked over to the driver's side window once more. Kissed him and said, "I'm so proud of you. I can't wait to hear how it goes today. I will let you know when I am home. I love you."

He looked at me with that please-don't-cry look and said, "I love you more."

Yes, a tear dropped out. I tried, I really did, and then I reminded him.

"Impossible. I love you More than More!"

The Bench

I sat on the bench inside the station. The sounds of motor mixed with the muffled words from the people next to me. They had no clue; my heart was breaking.

July 25, 2017

One more for the road, a bittersweet "I will see you later" and the beginning of the beautiful tomorrows to come. My heart is betwixt. So full of gratitude for this son of mine's strength, and his undeniable belief in the power of healing mind, body, and spirit as the path to true healing.

I sat there in the train station, in tears, and in pride, and now, a runny nose. My reflection is deep, soul-penetrating.

I love you. Josiah. Thank you to the abundance of friends and family for your love.

I posted these words with our last picture.

Sobbing now. Those muffled voices catching sight of my brokenness.

We had made it to the other side.

He...

Was...

Healing...

One More Sacred Moment

I would be given one more visit. One more sacred moment.

After Josiah was settled into his new role at Apple, he wanted to fly down to show his father and I that he was doing well. Our concerns for his health had continued. And he was determined to show us we could let go of those pangs.

He flew to his father's first. Mitchell would confirm that he did seem better. But there was a silence in his voice only I could hear. The apprehension from the fierce summer that had tried to steal our boy.

We were committed to stand in the faith that Josiah lived in.

I waited impatiently for my turn; two days that felt like an eternity. I made sure I had plenty for him to eat, and reminded myself he was on the mend.

Let the vibes of the summer go. Enjoy your time with him, I chanted to myself.

I tight-roped my days with him. Balancing my fears with my faith, as I had been doing for nine years. He was doing better! I wanted him to thrive and not have to deal with this anymore.

Luckily for me, he had an agenda and had our days full.

He wanted to go out to Joshua Tree to visit John the Flute maker.

We picked up Valerie, and off we traveled, through the giant stones of the desert scenery.

It had been some time since John and his wife Cathy had seen Josiah. Without words, their eyes spoke of their awareness. They could see how he had braved the summer's villain.

They fed us and off to the flute room Josiah, John and Valerie fled. What had John created that Josiah may want? When they returned, Valerie was over the moon. Her brother had let her help him pick out his next perfect flute. Thinking it would be his, forever. Never, hers.

I feel like Josiah knew. Like he felt the shifting from a higher consciousness. That place within your own spiritual awareness. Where the human mind does not quite understand, but knows.

It is always bittersweet to say goodbye at the healing home of John the flute maker. The spiritual and emotional basket they send you home with is so full. Yet you hold out the basket, just in case one more morsel of wisdom may befall from John or Cathy. You do not want to leave without it.

Mother & Son
September 28, 2017

Yesterday I said I would miss you as I dropped you off to fly back home.

With a slight glance you kissed me.
Your love poured through you.

Tears filled my eyes, with the sappy exits you always got from me.

You knew I would hold my breath until you were home.

Mother and Son.

I do not feel well

You are healing

Guess what, Mom.

Tell me everything

What do you think, Mom?

I will guide you

I am hungry,

I will feed you

I need you, Mom,

I am right here

I believe I can fly,

I will fly with you

Mother & Son

The Atmosphere

The following day, I had to deliver my son to the airport. To the giant steel contraption that would transport him back up north and once again out of my reach.

"No need to park, Mom," he told me.

It is true. At Ontario airport you cannot go in, sit and watch the planes ascend into the atmosphere.

He would check in and go up the escalator and that would be it.

I opened the hatch of my car and he took out his bags.

My eyes were erupting as he told me, "Stop, don't cry. I will be back in a couple months."

Knowing my tears hurt him also, I sucked it up like any good mom would do. I would save my blubbering for the ride home.

"I'll be back soon. I will call you as soon as I land." He kissed my forehead and turned. I watched him walk towards those huge sliding glass doors as they opened like a spacecraft.

Josiah glided through them as they were sliding shut. Robotically distorting my view.

Home

I had barely made it home myself when the phone rang. He had landed and was taxiing towards the airport.

Funny how you are not aware you are holding your breath. Until you exhale.

An hour later and he was home and making plans for his next visit, the early part of December.

"Why do we focus on manifesting money? Instead we should focus on manifesting love. Loving every cell in your body can be hard to do. Once you do love yourself, you also find that there is always food on your plate, water in your glass, a roof over your head, and peace in your heart. How can we love others if we do not love ourselves? Stop, breathe, look, and feel what is around you, and shine your light to the world."

~ Josiah "Akoya" David

Part III

The Alchemy of Josiah

"We are gifts from the heavens. We are all here for each other. Everything we need has been placed in our path at every step along the way."

~ Josiah "Akoya" David

The Earth Shifts

The challenges before us today,

are the challenges behind us tomorrow.

Moving us ever closer to clarity.

Every day greets us with challenges.

Some small. Some big.

But when we greet them back, head on, responding in
our integrity.

That challenge turns liquid,

and we move through.

We become stronger

Coping doesn't seem as difficult.

The earth shifts.

The next road appears.

And the journey continues.

Our wisdom.

And our direction.

Are birthed through the essence

of our experiences.

Through our own clarity.

Wisdom breaks free.

Raina**

2006

October 20, 2017

I awoke to the sound of my own voice screaming. My husband, carefully shaking me to come out of whatever was happening beyond my dream state.

I am a heavy dreamer. It is common for me to be so deeply interwoven with my dream that it collides with my outer world. Sometimes I am in full laughter. Gasping, trembling, and all too often, crying.

This time it was terror.

I was dreaming Rich and I were driving on the freeway, Rich behind the wheel. In front of us was a semi-truck driving at high speed, until it began to jack-knife. We were heading straight towards our demise. In the dream, I covered my eyes with my hands and spoke.

"Rich, we are going to see Heaven today. We are going to see Heaven."

This was the evening before Richard's daughter's wedding rehearsal dinner. The entire family, both his daughter's and her groom's, would be coming to our home for this dinner. With that on the agenda, I had to put this dream, and the intensity of it, back to sleep for later reckoning. Getting ready for his only daughter's wedding had to take precedence, of course. However, "Let's drive slow and watch out for semis!" I warned, as we took his mother to visit a friend the following day.

Rich used to think dreams are just that. Dreams. A manifestation of your subconscious. I believe they are messages. Especially when they impact your waking mind.

This dream and the dreams to follow would change his thoughts. Forever.

Juggernaut

The wedding was on Saturday, Oct 21. With the chaos of prior days now calm, I could finally think about that dream that had deeply impacted me, as we made the fifteen-minute drive to the chapel.

I googled the meaning of a jackknifed semi and found several. Overburdened, or about to be over-burdened, was one of them. *"The truck is a creation of your unconscious mind,"* I read, *"There is something in your life that you are facing, or soon will be facing, that you would rather avoid. Heed the wisdom of your inner mind; there is really no way out of this juggernaut."*

Juggernaut? I looked this up too. It means a huge, powerful, and overwhelming force. As we rode to the chapel, I was evaluating what this juggernaut in my dream could be. I also read that a crash indicated a disruption in your family life, and that it would take all your strength. At the time, I had several projects going on besides this wedding and Josiah's health. So, yes, I was a bit overburdened.

I read this out loud to Rich. No reply. He was fo-cused on getting to the wedding of his daughter. So, okay, I was left to navigate this myself. Maybe the timing for my projects were off. Maybe they were going to take too much of my time? I was so looking forward to creating something new, so why does that have to take a backseat? And what was beyond my strength and abilities...? The undercurrent of Josiah's health issues. But this made no sense. He was healing. Why would the Universe be telling me that something I was doing, or going to be doing, was going to interrupt my projects?

Interfere with my family and sap my strength? I dove inside my head. *Breathe. The wisdom here is; You need to pace yourself. Continue to stay in faith for his health, and take care of yourself, so you don't hit head-on into this semi!* I cautioned myself, as the word Juggernaut continued to flood my mind.

Sensing

The following day we had one remaining wedding task to complete: Drive to Menifee, an hour away, to watch the newlyweds open their presents.

I was acutely aware of what was missing during these full days: my daily conversations with Josiah. As we ventured back to the wedding party festivity, I sensed myself a bit outside the family conversations. I could see the gifts and feel their revel, but I needed to speak to my son. What had he been doing? How was he feeling? I was counting the moments when we could leave, and I could talk with him.

Finally, the gifts were all opened. The food had been eaten. All that was left was the mingling. I looked around the room. I have been with Rich for ten years now, but a stranger to the family I was with. I needed to return to my daily talks with Josiah, the conversations that tethered me to him, and made me feel aligned. I was uneasy and ready to go. I was sensing an urgency to call Josiah. An almost knowing that he was wanting to speak to me at that moment. But Rich was assigned tuxedo duty, and we now had to return them. One more hour to the tuxedo store, and then a fifteen-minute drive from there to home. I was getting anxious. I couldn't call from the car with Rich and his mother there. That would not give Josiah and I the time we needed; I would wait until I got home.

Why didn't I text him?

The Earth Shifts

I was finally home and could now resume what I knew to be my daily routine. But first things first. I put my purse down, went to do what we all need to do when we get home from a long journey, then walked back into the kitchen to retrieve my phone and call Josiah. That's when I saw I had a Facebook message from his friend Margot. Before I even looked at her words, I knew something was off. There was no reason for her to contact me. I clicked on the message.

Raina... What is your number?

An immediate panic overtook me as I typed the digits, then waited for the reply.

Josiah took a spill on the motorbike. He is in the hospital. We do not have any more information. We are trying to call the hospital.

What hospital? Call Me! I typed as desperation continued to consume its way through me. Josiah and Margot's husband Jesse had been out riding their motorcycles. Jesse was a couple miles ahead and had gone back to find Josiah when he did not arrive at their destination point. When he got there, he found paramedics already on the scene, caring for my son.

I answer the phone mid-ring; it's Jesse on the other

end. "Where is he? What is the name of the hospital?"

Rapidly wearing out the floor from my agitated pacing, I write the number and I am off the phone with Jesse and ringing this hospital that must have saved Josiah's life. I am about to hear Josiah's voice. That was what my heart was saying. But my soul knew different.

"Raina, maybe this is good," Rich said hopefully as he mimicked my pace, "Now that Josiah is in the hospital. This will be a chance for them to help him with his health. Maybe it is a good thing."

The hospital line put me on hold three times and three times I was disconnected.

"No! No! No! This is not good. This is not good," I cried, as I called back and begged them not to put me on hold. "I am hundreds of miles away, please, my son was in a motorcycle accident! Please tell me how he is!"

The receptionist calmly said, "Don't hang up, the doctor will be right with you."

I labored to breathe as my tears made their way down my face, creating a pool of disbelief on the floor. The doctor came on the line.

"We tried to revive him for an hour but could not save him."

That is when I turned to dust. I completely vanished, except for my hand that held the phone to my ear, that would not allow this voice to continue. I handed the phone to Rich and walked outside. The only thing that mattered now was finding him. I had heard him calling me as I sat, filled with angst, in that family gathering! He had wanted to talk with me right then, but it was from the ethers. I had felt him as he left his physical body!! Within seconds, a deep loud roar of yearning, mixed with uncomfortably numb torment, welled from my shredded heart.

"Josiah! Josiah! Josiah! Where are you? Where are you? Where are you, son? Show me where you are?"

That was all I wanted to know.

I had crashed straight into that jackknifed semi-truck. This was my juggernaut. I was going to see Heaven today. I was going to find him.

Invisible

What is happening to me?

I cannot feel my legs and I am not sure where I am. Everything is unfamiliar. I do not recognize anything. I hear Richard's voice, but I cannot understand what he is saying. Everything has slowed down, including my body, that is giving way and collapsing towards the hard cement beneath my feet. I am fainting. That is what is happening to me. Or, I am dying. I am dying. There is no way I am still alive. My heart has stopped with his, and I can't feel anything. Richard catches me and guides me to the ground. Yet I do not know how he saw where I was. I was invisible.

"Raina, Raina, sit. Let me prop you against this wall. You need to call Mitchell!"

Oh, my flipping Gawd! I need to do what? I have to tell someone else? I have to break the heart of his father? His siblings? Is my crushed soul not enough? I took my phone from his steady hand. I looked at it like it was a foreign object I had never seen.

"Take a deep breath. You are unraveling, Raina. This is something you cannot postpone."

I had to find my voice within me.

My automatic response in a crisis, well, with anything and all things, is to call my sister.

We, the last two of our parent's four children, had become one person in the last years of my mother's life. Taking on the different roles that would be one complete entity, the one our mother needed, to take care of her. So, it was my biological response to call her first.

"Sheri!" I know my voice was unrecognizable to her ears. I believe she began to cry before my voice ever told her the news. I was so confused. I didn't know if I would leave in the next five minutes to travel the five hundred miles to him, or if I was going to disintegrate. I told her I would call her back. I needed to call Mitchell and the kids.

I believe I was standing when I called Sheri. Pacing. But as my phone rang Mitchell, I had collapsed to the ground again.

"Mitchell!" I moaned as tears splashed his soul through the phone. "Josiah!"

To be honest, I do not know what I said. I am sure I told him about the accident. All I remember is my body pressed against the wall that supported my arms so the phone could exist near my face, long enough to tell him. Then I heard his cry. His torment embraced mine. And together the power of Josiah's love consumed us.

Jeremy. The Strength of my life. My firstborn, who without fail always answers his phone when I call. I could not believe what I was about to tell him. To hear his heart's cries deafened me.

"Can you come here?" I asked, unable to conceal my heart-wrenching cry.

"Yes, Mom, I will be right there."

"Hurry, Jeremy. Hurry."

Valerie. How am I going to tell My Beauty? Her heart is so tender. I did everything I could to compose myself, but my cry tore right through her.

"Mom. Mom. You are lying to me! "You're lying. Tell me you are lying!" Then her protests turned to begging.

Oh, how I wished I could have told her this was a cruel joke I was playing. That today, of all days, I had become a monster. But she knew me better than that. I had never. I would never.

Who was lying, was this world, without words. This was the cruelest expression of life. The joke was on me. On us.

"Come quickly, Beauty."

"I will be right there, Mom."

Still unstable, I called my sister back. I knew I was not going anywhere until we figured out our next step. At least I could share that. When she answered she informed me she was already halfway to my house from her home in Orange County, and a calm momentarily washed over me.

***

It was a tree after all. A tree, that "The Ethereal" had chosen from the beginning. Josiah was determined – no, adamant – that he would not fall prey to cancer. Maybe he knew all along, from before he came here, that cancer was not going to be the portal.

Maybe deep in our subconscious, we are all more attuned to the authentic truth that is within us.

"Open your heart, stand strong and balanced in your field.

Walk with clear direction.

Know the truth of you shines in every step."

~ Josiah "Akoya" David

Awareness

Known to me, in the silence of my mind.

There stood the answers.

In the chatter, I could not hear.

The stirring and the whirling kept me from understanding.

That I alone know me.

That the directions I take are mine.

That no one can control my destination.

Unless, I allow them to.

And then, my life is really not my own.

But given over.

And I live unhappy.

Known to me.

I take responsibility for my actions.

My life is created by my heart's intention.

And what I desire becomes reality.

Raina (1995)

Grief knocks you to the ground.

And when it hurts the most

I must believe – no, I know! –

He is with me.

The Sacred Alchemy of Josiah

So many signs began to come. And in so many unusual ways. As the days, weeks and months continued, I realized Josiah was showing up in a multitude of ways. My Elf Alchemist was the same in Spirit as he was here. And of course, he would challenge me to find him in his Alchemy. His multi talents still thriving from the other side.

Oracle

For four days my home had been turned into a refuge. A place where those who loved Josiah, and his family, could come and pay homage. Sunday to Wednesday blurred together, with the faces, within those days.

Wednesday evening, my friend Debbie and her husband brought pizza for the family. It was late afternoon, and the sun was still out on this warmer October day. We were sitting outside when she noticed a magenta glow surrounding my bewildered energy. Then she softly reminded me to put rose oil over my heart. Rose essential oil has the highest vibration of all the flowers and has the essence of Divine Love. As she spoke these words, a butterfly flew between us, circled, and whisked away. It took us both a second to catch our breath. But we both knew. Someone in Spirit, with their pure energy, can influence insects and animals, allowing them to show us they are here. The butterfly, and that beautiful "magenta" glow was, without question, Josiah.

Later that evening he confirmed his presence.

After four days, my sister had finally mustered up the courage to leave me for the night and make her way back home to Orange County. Rich was exhausted and fell asleep the instant the house went silent.

I wanted to find Josiah.

I made my way to my healing room – his, and my, favorite place in my house. Anytime he was back home he wanted to be on my massage table. As much as he loved me giving him my vibes, I knew it was he, gifting me his vibes, in those times. I mean, what adult son lets his mom put her hands all over him, unless she is giving him a facial/reiki session that ends with a kiss on the forehead? My signal to him that he could open his eyes.

I sat on the floor embracing the much-needed silence. I remember looking around the room thinking he would appear. Because, of course, I am dreaming, right? Then the flood began to arrive. There were no droplets of tears I could catch. They overturned my requests to stop. Continuing until I laid my head down on his scarf, which I had wrapped around my neck. A calm rushed through me. I sat back up and could feel him guiding my hand. I picked up two decks of oracle cards: Keepers of the Light by Kyle Gray and Talking to Heaven by James Van Praagh.

"What do You want me to do with them, Josiah?" I knew I had to pick one from Keepers, then one from Talking to Heaven, and repeat.

Card 1: *Charity, Prayer, and Contemplation: Connect to heaven, ask and you shall receive.* There I was, in the picture. It was a woman, praying to heaven, a magenta glow all around her and roses in her hair! Exactly what Debbie had described.

"JOSIAH!" I cried.

Card 2: *"I have a new understanding."* Of course, you do, son. You could always understand everything from a higher perspective. I felt as if I was in conversation. I asked him to tell me more!

Card 3: *The Shekinah, Sacred Self: Unleash your Spirit, your gifts, Dance to the sacred rhythm of life.* Shekinah means divine presence; Josiah was telling me to unleash my Spirit and my gifts. That we are in a new dance. A sacred rhythm towards divine presence.

Card 4: *We are so connected.* WE ARE SO CONNECTED! In truth, this was really all I needed to hear...

This message was so clear, I needed to stay focused in prayer and contemplation. Meditate and I would find him. It was a done deal. He already understands where he is, and he would show me. I just needed to stay true to my sacred self. Embrace my spirit, so we could find our sacred dance...

And Mom, by the way, we are so connected. Nothing can break this bond!

Call me crazy, but this was crystal clear to me. And as I continued this journey with him, these cards, especially the Talking to Heaven deck, continued to be a way Josiah could easily connect with me. So much so, I created a deck for us called Sacred Alchemy. Now, I am not telling you to use cards every day with every thought to connect to your child. They are a tool, and you will know instinctively when you should use them. You will feel it, deep within your soul.

Mom, Breathe. Hone in on your own truth. See them

for what they are, accepting of what is real and true for you. Now take it to the next level and open up to your senses, what is outside of you. Use your higher senses, Mom, see with your heart!

Butterfly Josiah

The next day, my sister-in-law Ginger and her husband arrived from out of state. A couple of my friends were over also. Jeanette, my friend from junior high, had brought dinner that evening. When she was ready to leave, I walked outside with her for a private minute to chat. I have three big trees that line the front of my house by the street. Our conversation led me to a memory – A reading I'd had with Carolan a few months prior. She had told me that I had a new spirit guide coming. Now, as I told Jeanette, I wondered if maybe that guide was Josiah.

As the words fell from my voice, we heard a rustling in the far-left tree. It was a huge butterfly, black and yellow. Our eyes locked in amazement, surprise and anticipation. Jeanette said to the butterfly, "Come closer, come closer." I joined in. This enormous butterfly flew to the middle tree, closer to where I was, spread open its wings and stopped. I actually kept my composure; I was captivated.

"Josiah, Josiah," I repeated. "I love you; I love you." I knew he had influenced this beautiful winged spirit. I continued to talk to it, the butterfly that housed Josiah.

One by one, my guests came to find me. Elicia, then Ginger. I told them about the spirit guide conversation

Jeanette, and I had shared. I had been out there for at least fifteen mins. All my kids and grandkids were in the backyard. I asked someone to go get them. They all quickly came until all of us were in unison with the Butterfly Josiah.

I started to really focus on it. What was this butterfly saying? What did Josiah want us to know? Then I saw it.

"Look," I told them, "the butterfly has a blemish on the right side of his wing and his left foot is missing, I think Josiah is showing us what happened to him. That the impact was on his right side and something happened to his left leg."

Jeremy, Valerie, Michael and the grandkids, were all committed to my vision. They saw it too. We were all taking pictures like professionals, but it was Valerie who stepped in so close and took the picture that clearly showed us what that blemish on the wing looked like. It was in the shape of a heart. Our minds were blown.

The night sky was upon us and a chill was in the air. We said goodnight to Butterfly Josiah, who was not going to leave us. I had held my tears long enough.

Now I could cry.

Can I Stay with You?

Once more, the house became silent as my children and grandchildren went home for the evening. Tomorrow was Friday. I was being forced out of the house to go to the mountains. Just ten minutes up the road, where we would have Josiah's celebration of his extraordinary life.

Leaving what I deemed the safety of the walls of my home made me uneasy, but the kids insisted. "You have to get out of the house." I did not want to cause a scene. And, I knew they still needed me too. But until tomorrow, I could once again cry myself to sleep and awake the same.

This night was different, however. I fell into a deep dream.

I dreamt I was at some sort of high school reunion. Possibly mine. Jeanette was there. She was wearing a white dress. Rich and I were sitting close to the door that led into the classroom area. The reunion was outside, and there were chairs against the walls, and round tables with chairs and people at them. Someone gave me a baby to hold. I got up to visit one of the round tables. I looked toward the classroom window. There in the window, inside the building, looking out at me, was Josiah, in his cap and gown with his sunglasses on. Just as he had worn them at his actual graduation. I fainted with the baby in my arms, but when I came to, I was still holding the baby. I started apologizing for fainting. I walked over to someone and gave them the baby, then I went back to where Rich and I were sitting, which was just to the right of where I had seen Josiah. Rich had hair all over him, like he had gotten a haircut. I got up again to go see Jeanette, and as I walked to her, a plane crashed right in the area where this reunion was. I ran over to the plane and told the pilot, "You are okay. You are okay. You did not fall far!" The scene changed and now Rich and I were outside in the schoolyard. There were small children walking towards us, like we were at an elementary school. A younger Josiah, eight or nine years old, came up to me and said, "Can I stay with you?"

To this day, as I write this, it is as clear as if it just happened. There is so much symbology:

High school can represent a time of transition, when you are transitioning from child to adult, with all its fears and challenges. Reunion represents a time of gathering. Jeanette in white, represented the spirit guide we had just spoken of. The baby, a sign of vulnerability and helplessness. I did give the baby back, which symbolizes that it was not going to stay within me forever. The plane crash, a sign of fear of the future, and the problems it may bring. A plane crash also means your life is seriously out of control. Oh, how it was! Yet I was able to tell the pilot that he was okay, he had not fallen far, all the while Josiah was watching from the window. Richard's hair cut comes in later when I find little hairs from Josiah's shaved face at his home. Then, we are outside, and my boy asks me, "Can I stay with you?"

Can you stay with me? Was that even a question? Your entire adult life I nearly begged you to stay with me! "Yes! Yes! Stay with me, Josiah! Stay with me forever!"

Dimes

Friday morning, I awoke blown away and shaken. Trying to digest the information from my dream to a consumable level. I quickly went over and over it. What in the world? So intense. I had seen my son without question. And he was staying with me. Though my plane was wrecked, and I was bleeding, he was telling me I had not fallen far. Or possibly, *he* hadn't.

Ginger and her husband Rick were up and ready for whatever I needed for the day. What I needed was to go back to sleep to see Josiah. But that was not going to be an option. Aimee, Jeremy's girlfriend arrived to swoop me up and take me to the mountain reception area.

I am a flip flop or boot kind of girl. My tennis shoes are only worn when I go walking, which I had not done since the summer. I thought they may be a better option for the day. As I lifted them to enter my foot, I saw a dime? A dime! How in the world would a dime fall into my shoe in the closet? Josiah?? Then, when I walked into the grandkid's playroom, a dime was on the floor. The guest room, two pennies and a dime on the floor. Then he took it to the next level. When I went into my healing room to gather what I would take with me on Saturday when I went to get Josiah. A DIME was laying on the massage table! Just to be clear, money is never exchanged in that room. And no one ever pays me in change. Yet there sat a single dime, waiting for me.

My son was making his presence known, placing dimes and pennies in places he knew I would find them. We have all heard the phrase, "pennies from heaven!" I knew Spirit could move and manifest objects and mess with electronics. Dimes made sense. Josiah had a "man hippie bag." The label on it: "Dime Bag."

With the dimes in hand I got in the car. Driving to Oak Glen was surreal. I was an invisible passenger to a destination that would do what? Celebrate my child that is where? In a monastery in the Himalayan mountains, right? Tell me I am still sleeping; somebody please wake me.

Caravan

Saturday finally arrived. For seven days I had one foot out the door. I just wanted to leave. "Please! Somebody take me to my child!", but nobody would. There was too much red tape, as they call it. I could not just go get him? Really? He is mine! But nope. I had to go through this, and go through that, and sign this and sign that. But today. Today I could go. The Universe was allowing me to proceed.

We caravanned up to Josiah's home in Santa Cruz. Three trucks. The siblings in one. Richard and I in ours, and Mitchell and his wife in theirs. Mitchell and I agreed we would wait for one another and go into his room together.

On the way up, out of the blue, one of Josiah's friends, Kelly, who was deeply connected to my son, private messaged me on Facebook. We conversed back and forth through these messages on the drive up. This was not only distracting but comforting to have someone who would speak to me only about Josiah, because that is all I could really talk about. He had come to her in a dream the night he left. He told her that it was a surprise. That one minute he was there on his motorbike and the next minute he was like...He repeated "a big surprise."

Kelly went on to describe her dream.

The road was a dusty dry dirt, with trees going around a curve. There was a motorcycle laying on its side in front of a tree. Josiah was standing with me. We were down the road looking at the scene. He was telling me the intensity of going through the veil so quickly... He was very matter of fact. He said it was shocking. Like surprising. An intense pressure. He "showed" me. I felt it in my body. He said he thought to go back into his body, but looked and realized it was not an option. He was very matter of fact about that too. Then he "showed" me our connection through time. Like a downloaded slideshow that I can still feel.

His Room

Driving through the curvy roads to Santa Cruz, towards his house, his room, where everything he owned existed, was daunting. My anxiety was in high gear as my heart raced, and tears fell, and yet, I still felt hollow. We parked and gathered to go in. Mitchell and I walked towards Josiah's room, which was downstairs, in this giant Victorian home. Solemnly, we opened the door. Both of us just standing there, mystified and breathless.

Within minutes our children came through the door. They had waited long enough. Now this tiny room was filled with all the love of his family. We all just looked and touched everything. I crawled up into his loft bed and laid there, with his jacket on, and his pockets filled with anything I could touch that was his.

Of course, right below his dresser, a dime. Outside his room one of his roommates had drawn a picture of him. Below his picture, a nickel, and a dime. His roommates had already set up an altar with all of Josiah's favorite treats, trinkets, and pictures of him. They had planned dinner and a gathering for us that night. The rest of that day is a little murky.

The Gathering

Twenty or so friends showed up to share stories about Josiah. Margot had been in the middle of creating a new drawing for her clothing line when Jesse and my son took that ride. She brought her drawing, a scarab, and presented it to us that night. She dedicated the design to Josiah, and the new line of clothing with that design, naming it "Akoya."

His roommate Brandon then revealed that he had written a song and wanted to sing it for us. I have no words to express how this made me feel, so let me let you feel what I did.

In our hearts we hold you so dear

Crashing waves, Remembering the days
Laughing Soul, always wanting more

His hands that heal, we know magic is real
Light so bright, Pierces through this night

In our hearts we hold you so dear
In our hearts we hold you so dear

Art of wood, Inspired the greatest good
Guide you home, You'll never be alone

In our hearts we hold you so dear
In our hearts we hold you so dear

Cause you're my friend
Until the end
I just wanted you to know

Sacred brother
Return to mother
The universe calls you home

You're still my friend

Through the end

I just wanted you to know

Sacred brother

Return to mother

The universe calls you home

I say hey Josiah, thank you Josiah

I say hey Josiah, thank you Josiah

I wish you were here, but I'm glad you are free

So grateful I knew you, You helped me see

Life is so precious, You can't go it alone

We're all so connected, And we'll rise as one

I say hey Josiah, thank you Josiah

I say hey Josiah, thank you Josiah

In our hearts we hold you so dear

In our hearts we hold you so dear

In our hearts we hold you so dear

In our hearts we hold you so dear

~Brandon Walton~

No Stone Left Unturned

The next morning, I woke with the words of Brandon's song penetrating my entire being. I was not surprised, yet still so blown away by the impact Josiah's presence had made on his housemates, in just over a year. Then, the realization that this is the morning we were traveling to the crash site, and I was finally going to lay eyes on my beloved child, crowded out the words of his song. How was I going to make it through this day? I silently cried, as the tears kept coming. *"We're all so connected, and we'll rise as one!"*

"Josiah!" I said in my mind. I could feel him through these words, as he covered my heart with them. I sat up, wiped my tears and made my way towards the shower; I knew he was waiting for me.

As soon as I arrived at Josiah's home, I walked into his room, and my shaman-like gypsy spirit took over.

I wanted to bring his elfin clothes to him, since he had been wearing motorcycle gear, and cover him in a beautiful blanket. Bring him certain things and have it a certain way.

I was going to make sure this was an event that honored the essence of the man my son is.

It was not like I planned anything. I did not really think it through. I just went into that supernatural grace I spoke of. My daughter began to witness my mind in action, and she synced with me, grabbing his flute as I grabbed sage. We were loading up our pockets again, with feathers, and crystals. We took his stuffed turtle that had traveled in every car he had ever owned, agreeing that it should travel the rest of the way into the ethers with him.

I had created a blend of essential oils called "One Love" the previous summer during his Healing Retreat time. He loved the name and everything about it, that also came with me.

Valerie grabbed the small round wooden dream-catcher he had been working on.

With our pockets loaded up, and our hearts frayed, we all gathered in our trucks and drove to meet Jesse.

We met off the 17, in between Santa Cruz and San Jose. Up in those mountains, I had just traveled through with my beloved child.

At the meeting place, we all huddled into two trucks. Jesse directed us which way to go. My body was tightening as we traveled up the windy road. I could sense how this drive would have been way too much for Josiah, given his physical condition at the time. And now in full distress, I kept repeating these words: "This was too much for him, this was too much for him!"

I wanted to scream out, "Why didn't somebody stop him?!" But what good would that do? Josiah did what Josiah wanted to do. And he had wanted to ride this motorcycle.

We passed the tree. Jesse's startled voice says, "Oh. It was right there. Turn right!" Startled ourselves, we turned to see a park right below the accident site.

I looked at this park, thinking, *Please, I pray this park was empty when he crashed,* but I do not know. I don't know anything.

We walked back to see the tree. See the curves of the road. The skid marks. Mitchell, Richard and Jesse walk up the road, trying to make sense of how the crash happened.

Jeremy, Valerie, Michael and I wandered around the grounds by the tree. Looking for evidence.

I lit the sage and feathered the smoke around the tree. Sending my prayers and love towards the sky. Then I held the tree. The last element that touched my baby. It held him now, and now it must hold me.

Michael found Josiah's gauged earring on the ground. Before the entire sentence – "Look what I found!" – was out of his mouth, Valerie, who has the same size gauged ears as Josiah, snatched it out of his hand and had it in her ear. Earrings were their jam. Josiah loved to give her the earrings he had replaced with something new, which made them even more priceless to her.

Valerie put lavender in the tree. Jeremy carved a J, and I found a ballpoint pen on the ground. I wished it had been a marker, but I didn't want to make the Earth feel bad. This is what She was giving us.

We all wrote on the tree as we said goodbye to this moment in time. A moment unwanted, but necessary.

As much as I wanted to hate the tree, I couldn't. Josiah had not died there. He had become one with the tree and went back to the forest. As all elves do.

I am genuinely good at twisting a situation with my rose-colored glasses. But this was a twist that would not ease my grief. It just eased my perception of the story.

The thought of him having a moment of fear was too much to bear. Later you will see how he tells me he ascended before the motorcycle embraced the tree. And that was exactly what I had thought that day, as I embraced the portal he chose to enter through.

"The Castle"

Now was the journey to the mortuary in San Jose. Why does Mortuary have to sound so grim. Can't they call it a Castle?

On the drive there, we talked about the crash site. What we thought we saw, or did not see. The earring. The pen. Branches we took. The broken site pole in the back of our truck. Bark. And what we left at the tree, the sacred mementos of our broken hearts.

When we arrived at the Castle, Laurie came out to greet us. She was a tall woman dressed in black, but not morbid black. It was beautiful black. Elegant black. She walked towards me like a goddess.

We had talked on the phone several times. I knew I was in good hands.

I gave Laurie his green elfin shirt and the blankets I had taken from his bed. The ones he would always wrap me in when I was with him.

There was no way I was walking in and seeing him covered in anything other than his colorful blankets, and that was that. Laurie did exactly as I instructed.

She guided us down the long hallway to the room.

The door opened and across the room lay my son. Perfect. Beautiful. Sleeping. My daughter, my watcher, walked arm in arm with me. I didn't know whether to run or walk slow.

I don't even know what I really did. I think we all walked at the same pace.

Valerie placed the wooden art on his chest, and we laid crystals and feathers inside of it. She put his flute in his hands. It was bizarre, surreal and numbing. He was just sleeping, right? Are you going to wake the f*#^ up? Wake up, Josiah!

Valerie was stroking his long brown hair. I looked up at Mitchell and said, "I want his hair." Richard had known that was going to happen, so his feet were already turned towards the door to ask for scissors. Valerie and I both had small hair ties in our hair. I pulled out mine and she pulled out hers and braided her brother's hair. Richard came back and gave Mitchell the scissors. He cut his hair and handed it to me, saying, "I remember how Josiah used your hair as his blanket as he sucked his thumb."

Now, his hair would be *my* blanket and my security.

When we walked in, I could see that the impact had been on the right side, just as the butterfly had shown us. Valerie asked Jeremy to check his legs. Jeremy lifted the blanket to see that his left leg had been wrapped, also shown to us by the butterfly. That was the moment when his three siblings realized Josiah was capable of communicating from where he was.

One Love essential oil blend also laid on Josiah's chest. Jeremy opened the bottle and rolled it across his arms. I grabbed Jasmine, which was Josiah's favorite, and put it on his mustache. He loved the smell of it. Then rose oil. I had a few other blends we rolled on him, sending him off with our healing oils.

I don't know how long we stayed there. An hour, maybe more. But there is a point where you know it is time to go. We gathered all the things we had brought for him, except his sea turtle. I told everyone I needed ten minutes alone with him. My daughter was apprehensive. She thought I might crumble. Rich assured her, "It's okay. Your mom will be okay."

At an outing with friends four years prior, one of them had played a CD by Jai-Jagdeesh. Every song moved my soul, but when I heard "In Dreams," I wept. Knowing Josiah's health wavered back and forth, it became my cry song. Now, it has become my prayer song. It starts with, "Know you are loved, rest in peace, dream your sweet dreams 'til your soul is released," and goes on to say, "Beloved child, my heart is yours."

I knew the song was seven minutes long. I needed ten.

As soon as everyone left, I grabbed my phone and played the song. Got as close as I could and sang every word to him. Crying. Holding. Loving. Reminding him. He is Loved. He *is* Love.

The song ended and Valerie reentered. She had given me my ten minutes but that was it. She put her arm around me. "Mom, it's time to go." I knew she was right. What more could I possibly do? I knew this was the last time I would lay eyes on my beautiful child. My likeminded son. My guru.

She turned me around like a ragdoll.

"I can't look back," I cried, "If I look back; I will go back!"

"Okay, Mom."

We walked toward the door as we had entered, arm in arm, like we were one person.

I did not look back.

The Summit

We went back to Santa Cruz to pack up Josiah's world and take it to mine.

It is such a crazy thing – how you can be so exhausted yet unable to sleep. Anxiety has its own adrenaline. Like caffeinated bubbles in your blood. Ready to explode at any time, with just a thought.

We packed up the rest of Josiah's belongings. I thanked his room, his housemates, and the owner of the home once more. These were the people with whom he had chosen to share the last part of his earthly story.

The siblings headed to San Francisco to have an adventure in honor of their brother. Richard and I waited for the phone call granting me permission to go and get my son.

We had hours before we would travel back to San Jose. We decided that we should take care of business, go to Josiah's bank, the post office, and AAA.

I felt like a complete liar as the words were falling out of my mouth. This could not be true. The sentences I was saying to these clerks, tellers, and agents, but they were true, and I had to say them.

Leaving AAA, we realized we were in the next town,

just south of Santa Cruz. I google-mapped the roads that would take us towards San Jose. Richard, who always likes to be ahead of the game, said, "What's the next turn?"

"We take this until we make a left on Summit," I directed.

"Summit!" he repeated, and I could tell his mind was questioning and piecing something together. Jesse had told us that he and Josiah took a back road that day, rather than going up the 17. Now Richard and I summed up that this must be the route. Of course, it was. Josiah wasn't going to leave me completely in the dark; he would take me on his last journey.

I began videoing the route. Then I thought, *Should I video? Should I not video? Do I take this in? Do I not take this in? Oh, my Gawd! This was the road he took. It was so curvy. He must have been so tired.*

My mind raced as I turned the video on and off. *Why didn't I call him that morning? Why hadn't we spoken? Would he have still taken this ride? Would he have told me he was going on the motorcycle?*

I didn't think so, because he knew how I felt. He knew I would throw a fit. And he would not want to go on a motorcycle ride right after he upset his mom. That would not have worked for him. He could not handle me being upset. "Don't get crazy on me, Mom!" he would say. So, I know that phone call was purposely omitted from the day. And from previous days. Because he would have told me. He told me everything. The best way for him not to tell me something was not to talk with me at all. Which had never happened until he borrowed this motorcycle!

As we drove along this road, my mind continued babbling and babbling, like water going over the most treacherous rock formations. My heart was racing. As we turned left on Summit, Richard asked, "Do you want to go back up to the site?" and, without hesitation, "Yes!" poured out of me.

Angel Wings

Now that it's just the two of us, we can be quiet. We can experience his full ride if we follow the roads to the tree. With all the curves and hills, this was a hell of a ride for anyone, let alone someone who had braved the summer's villain as Josiah had, and who had not ridden a motorcycle for a long while. Well, this was a lot. It was a lot to take in. When we arrived back up at the tree, Rich assessed the roads again, gathering a second perspective.

I went to the tree. Looked at the carved "J" and our writings. Lavender was still hugging itself to it. I looked around, digging through the debris, to see if I could find anything else. Was there just one thing of his that we had missed? Coming out of the debris and standing by the side of the road, I looked back at where his body had lain. The sun was shining through the trees, casting shadows everywhere. I could see the sun's outline on the brush. I blinked my eyes a few times to make sure I wasn't seeing things. The sun's rays through the leaves had created ANGEL WINGS! Angel wings? At the exact place where he was laying just a week prior?

Of all the times of the day when the sun could come out, and shine its glory through the trees, and create Angel wings, it had done so the moment I was standing there. I knew it was Josiah.

I was completely awestruck as we continued our drive, to get my baby from the goddess Laurie.

Owl Energy

With my son on my lap as I promised him, I carried him all the way home.

We arrived there at midnight, tired and fatigued.

I opened the truck door and heard the wrestling of the trees, and the most bizarre squawking noise. I had never heard it before!

"Richard, what is that noise?"

"It is the owl," he tells me, "from the backyard."

That owl had never been in the front yard before, and I had never heard it make so much noise. But, on this night, as I opened the truck door, Josiah had influenced the elements, and the owl had come to the front to greet us. The symbols from birds are many, but tonight and in the days to come they were representing immortality, and spirit messages from Josiah. He was with us. He was home.

Birds

Now it was time to prepare for the "Celebration." This what? Celebration? Did someone slip me something hallucinogenic, and I am in a nightmare?

I had to write something. Everyone insisted that I did not have to talk. Yes, I did. I was the only one who could put into words what he meant to me.

I was mystified as we drove the fifteen minutes to the chic hidden wedding venue where Aimee worked. Her boss had graciously allowed us to have *it* there. *It.* The memorial? The service? The ceremony? Celebration? I couldn't name it. All I knew was, if it had to happen, this mountain paradise was where it had to be.

I didn't plan a thing. It was like magic when I arrived. Aimee had taken care of everything.

People began to trickle in. People I had not seen in a very long time. People who had been through thick and thin with me since I was a teenager. People. People. And more people.

Grateful to see them. But dazed. I was under a spell. The spell of disbelief and denial.

The scene was set with rainbow roses Valerie had created and arranged. Magnificent bouquets to honor her brother and his colorful array of talents and magical abilities. The garden setting was lush and green with tall forest trees surrounding the patio.

First, Josiah's father spoke. Then, one by one, his friends and family came. Their hearts and stories depicting the impact Josiah had had on them. Suddenly, a brilliant teal bird began to chirp. Louder and louder, catching the attention of the crowd. Valerie was standing behind me to the side. She grabbed my shoulders to point out the bird that had already stolen my attention. He was here. I looked at my like-minded friends, who were all sitting together, and spoke with my eyes.

Do you hear that?

They nodded in astonishment. *Oh, yes!*

Then he flew to the back tree, where I believe he was met with other family birds. My mom, dad, sister and brother. Mitchell's mom and grandma too. I couldn't tell how many birds were squawking, but there were several. The messages continued. My grandkids. Valerie. Isabella. Rain. And John the Flute maker serenaded us. Then it was my turn. I wanted to go last in case I could not brave my way through it.

I knew I would not be able to stand, so I brought a stool from home. I had a whole roll of paper towels. Not Kleenex. I knew I would overflow if I started with even one tear.

I looked down at the words I had written, then looked up to the trees. The birds had gone silent. The butterflies were still, and my body softened, as if he had sat down on my lap to compose me.

I looked over at my daughter. She was aware of the silence, as was everyone.

It was as if Josiah was directing the crowd, saying, "Shush, everyone. My mom is about to read. I need to help her!"

Then I opened my mouth, and completely composed, told these beautiful friends of his, and mine, his story.

His Tribute of/to His Life

When I was pondering what I would write, say, or how that could be possible, my whole body would spin.

How am I going to form words to write on paper? How am I going to create anything that could describe him?

So, I took a deep breath and then I asked Josiah "What do you want me to do? What do you want me to say?"

And I heard him say, "Drink water. You need to drink water, Mom. You are dehydrated!" He was right of course, so I filled up his water bottle. Took an enormous drink. And asked again. and I heard him say...

"Tell My Story. I know you cannot tell it all. But make them laugh. Share my triumphs and my love."

Before I was ever pregnant, Mitchell and I knew we would have a son named Josiah David. No ultrasounds ever. So, every birth was a surprise. A few weeks before I was due with my first child, Spirit spoke and told me/us this was not Josiah. That this gift was Jeremy, "My Strength," and he is.

And again, I became pregnant, and I wondered if this was Josiah. And again, Spirit spoke and said no. I have another gift for you – Valerie, "My Beauty," and she is. And I was pregnant again, and I pray with all my might: Please let this be Josiah.

I am kind of over being pregnant. And this time Spirit replied, Yes. I am giving you Josiah, "My Healer," and he is.

Josiah's younger years were comic relief. He was a funny, funny boy. Full of theatrics and costumes.

For a season of time, it was cowboy boots. Cowboy hat. A cape and shorts. And not just one pair of shorts, but multiple pairs at a time. Possibly for that quick change to perform. One day I walked into his room, he was around five years old, and he was laying on the floor like a woman trying to zip up those pants that just don't fit anymore. He was trying to get his fifth pair of shorts on! I said, "Josiah, why do you need five pairs of shorts on?" he said, "I just want to!" And this became the theme of how he lived his entire life: "I just want to!"

Josiah's love for music started young also. He wanted drums, a guitar, and a flute, of course, just to name a few. He could articulate his heart early on, through pictures and words. We even had our own language, some may say it was babble, but we completely understood each other. When he was around twelve-ish, we went to see the great Y circus in Redlands. His entire world shifted. That was it, he was in. That was all he wanted to do, and he was good at it. His creative valve had been turned on full blast. Juggling, clowning, tumbling. One year, he was so excited that he could do these amazing flips in one of the performances that he refused to tell me what he would be doing in the show, and wouldn't let me come watch the rehearsals, because he wanted to surprise me. And in amazement, we all watched him with so much pride. Yes, because of what he was doing, but more because he loved what he was doing. And this love guided him straight into college, to the theater arts and into theater design. And while in college he got that job everyone wants: Disneyland. Dressed up for the Alice in Wonderland float in the parade of dreams, he bounced on that trampoline. Off and on the float, his hilarious facial expressions, the ridiculous antics. I felt more joy from his joy than I could ever feel from my own, and like a crazed fan I would follow the parade just to continue to watch. He was always pushing the limits and stretching the boundaries. Breathing fire, spinning his Cyr wheel like a magical coin that transcended time and space, and flying into an audience on two red ribbons like a bird in flight, he mesmerized us always and often.

On August 17, 2008, two days before his twentieth birthday. The earth shifted and a new road appeared. Josiah was diagnosed with Hodgkins Lymphoma. Nothing was very funny anymore. It was a ten-day hospital stay, with a very scary doctor. The conclusion rocked our world, rocked his world, and in that moment, Josiah went from a Yuppie to a Hippie. It did something to him internally like I had never seen. His direction changed. He sought to find his soul's purpose. His art shifted and he became limitless in his possibilities. His first venture was out to Joshua tree where he built a home on top of a boulder, it's true. He would work through his emotions by painting, writing and seeking out the healing arts. He dove deep into the meaning of life, curious on all aspects and what all the world, and worlds, has to say about Spirit. He looked to everything holistic to heal his body, and the bodies of anyone he encountered. He looked to everything Spiritual to heal his soul, and any souls that graced his presence. And he looked to unconditional love to heal the wounds of his heart, and the hearts in need of healing. And again, his art morphed into wooden wonders, masterpieces of geometric design, curls and swirls of absolute healing magic.

The evolution of Josiah was incredible to watch, and to experience...

He did keep cancer at bay. He traveled. He continued to entertain with his rainbow of talents. He studied everything he could on healing cancer, healing emotions and healing hearts. He created mystical art that lives and breathes on their own, captivating your vision with every loving detail. And he loved, with purity. If he didn't like or understand a situation, he would rant, but the ranting was to dissect and move through it, to bring it full circle, and back to love. And he healed, with his words, unfiltered, with raw wisdom, that streamed from pure intention. If you were watching him perform, his light would radiate towards you, and you could feel it. If you have a piece of his art, I barely need to say anything, for the love and the precision he put into these pieces are without question, infused with an energy unlike any other. And the touch of his healing hands, well, his clients would say he was a magician...

The last couple of years, Lymphoma reared its ugly head again, but my son Josiah's belief system was stronger than his will to be defeated.

That childhood determination to get that fifth pair of shorts on was stronger than ever. Whatever it took. One leg, then another, laying on that floor wiggling his body until every thread of fabric would layer upon the next, that is how he was going to survive. Nothing was going to stop him. He made his belief his truth, and his truth was he was healed, and he is...

There was a reason I named my kids, Beauty, Strength, and Healing. I thought I was going to teach them what that means. But no, they have taught me what that means...

In the twenty-ninth year of my life I gave birth to Josiah, and in the twenty-ninth year of his, he birthed in me a calling I am not even aware of yet.

I have spent every day since my beautiful son transitioned looking through his art, his words, his life. And everywhere I look I see trees. Trees in the atmosphere. *Trees with him almost inside of them. Trees next to cliffs. Trees, trees, and more trees. And the tree of life, well it was a huge part of him, so huge he tattooed it on his chest. A few years back he bought me a book called, The Tree in Me. And the irony that this beautiful boy of mine, this magical, mystical and somewhat mysterious man, would gravitate towards a tree in that final moment, as if he became it. Well, it has twisted my mind into trying to find something that I can make sense of. Something more supernatural. For he could find the beauty in everything and I know he would want me to find his Spirit through my pain. Am I angry at the tree? Oh yes. I have a gamut of unexplored feelings I have yet to embrace. But I trusted Josiah with all my heart in this life, and I must continue to trust him, so we can find Our own language again, our babble, and he can come back, and be with me...*

Every year at the anniversary of his diagnosis, I write him some profound Mommyism.

Two years ago, I wrote him this:

I have spent every moment of this day in gratitude

For You Josiah

We Weave through The Tapestry of Our lives, each thread colored with experience. Each experience forming a pattern. Each pattern a decoration of where we have been, who we are and where we will journey...

You My Amazing Child have woven a tree...

The tree of

"Your" Life ... and it is Perfect.

My Hope and My prayer is that what Josiah has woven with you takes root, and that the impact of his tapestry is healing to your own Tree of Life.

Josiah would want you all to be healed, to be whole, to play, to dance, to create. But most of all, Josiah would want you to Be Love...

My Heart, My Soul, My Spirit, My Love will never be the same,

It will be Stronger,

Because of Josiah.

"Healing occurs when the light from above fills our being, transforming the light within, allowing us to shine a brighter light into the world."

~ Josiah "Akoya" David

Portland

Josiah's Portland tribe was also having a gathering that Sunday.

I wanted to travel the thousand miles to be there with them. The people he had called his soul family. No one wanted to tell me not to go, for fear I would crumble. Yet they knew. Going would be what did the crumbling.

My nephew Joel, who lives in Southern Oregon, told me he would go with me if I needed him. Rain told me she would drive me, and Elicia told me she would buy the tickets to fly there, arrange the hotel and make sure we have a car. All I had to do was go. But my tired mind and body knew even that would be too much.

Rain said she would skype me in at four p.m. that Sunday.

After our gathering that Friday, and twenty-four hours of crying, I pulled myself together to take part in OneDoorlands celebration for my son and their beloved friend.

Beloved

At exactly four o'clock, I sat on the floor of my living room, computer open, still feeling like I had been hit with a nuclear bomb. Rain connected me. One by one, Josiah's people came to the computer to talk with me. They told me stories of their boundless love for him.

The actual event would start at six. I watched the screen as each one came to the altar of pictures, crystals, candles, and art that Josiah had created. I witnessed them offering their love as well as obtaining his. I was jolted out of the event when I heard a knock at my door. It was Elicia!

"I just wanted to stop by and check on you."

"Rain has me skyped into Portland!" I told her. We took the laptop back into my spare bedroom. Shut the door and began to experience more love, authenticity, vulnerability, and creative expression than I had ever experienced in my entire life. They continued to pass Rain's laptop around the room, each talking directly to me as they spoke of their personal and profound experiences with Josiah. Faces, put to the stories he had told me about over the years, breathing life through the screen and penetrating my heart. I stayed on with them until the very end. Almost midnight.

Elicia had wanted to make sure I was completely taken care of if I decided to go to Portland. She mysteriously showed up at the moment this amazing gathering started and did indeed take care of me. Cried with me. And was profoundly changed by the experience. As was I.

Blurred lines

It's a new dimension I'm living in now. Everything runs together. What was once a mindless task is now an anxiety-ridden chore. Going to the store is like swimming in the middle of the freezing ocean with sharks surrounding me.

Driving. I should not be allowed to drive. I cannot see through the tears. I just want to stay home where I am safe, or so I think.

I must let Rich get back to his life. I must be alone in this house. I have to understand something, anything. Because right now, nothing makes sense. Except being with those grandkids of mine. That makes sense. So, I can get back to that. But, oh, right, I must drive to get them. Can I do that? I can do that, if that is all I do, then that will be enough.

It had only been three weeks when I endeavored to pick up my grandsons from school. *Hold it together!* I told myself as I drove towards my house, boys in tow. But I cannot abstain. The tears begin. Both look at me in wonderment. "Why are you crying, Grandma?' and in the same breath they answer themselves, "Oh. Josiah!"

I cannot hide it, and maybe that is okay. I do not want them to think that I am not grieving. That somehow, it is OKAY that Josiah is not here. This is part of life and these emotions are real, and raw, and true. But they are children and they do not need to take care of me.

I quickly responded. "Yes, Josiah. I miss him so much. This is hard. Grandma is sad, but I am happy when I am with you."

This became my mantra to them. They understood that Josiah is a huge part of me. They understood so well that they embraced Josiah's afterlife abilities with me. They also knew that when I am with them, I am happy. This gave them the ability to see grief as love, spirit, sadness and joy. And the way it blends, all at the same time.

November 22. 2017: One Month

Nancy and I had a trade set up for November, but I was in no shape to trade anything. Nancy came anyway, knowing I could use her energy. The night before she came, I had woken up in the middle of the night, hearing the word *ancestry*. I thought to myself, Ancestry.com? Where in the world did that come from? Then I heard another phrase, *Put it behind you!* It didn't make sense to me, but even as I wrote it down, I knew in my soul that it did not mean what I had written, it meant something else.

Nancy arrived to see her tattered friend, desperately needing to lay on my healing table and receive her love. Nancy's wisdom comes fluently. She begins telling me things that Spirit is saying. Then she says, "Josiah wants you to get in touch with your ancestry." My ancestry?! I had not told her about waking up with these words. In that moment I knew I had lived in many lifetimes with Josiah. He was letting me know we had always been together.

She went on to tell me, "Josiah is anxious for you to let go of his earthly life and connect with him in Spirit."

I began to weep, repeating, "Why is he rushing me? Why is he rushing me?" Yet I knew that this was what I was hearing when I heard "put it behind you!" That was so Josiah! He was impatient here on earth, so it makes sense he would be impatient with me to get to the next level! With tears streaming down the sides of my face, I pleaded, "You've got to give me time, Josiah! You're asking too much of me!"

The next morning, I sat in silence. Pondering why he

was rushing me to put it behind me. To let go of what we had here, as if he thought I was so capable of switching gears that fast. This was going to take time. I desperately wanted him to call me from here, not from the ethers. I grabbed my pen and wrote this.

Today I sit here in silence. Waiting for you to call and tell me about some new adventure you are going to undertake. Something so creative my mind is blown once more.

And it was never because you wanted to create money. Always because you wanted to create LOVE, and Healing. I know you want me to hurry up, I know you understand where you are. It is just too soon, Josiah; it is just a month today. Give me a sign you are here.

I wrote these words and then the phone rang. It was Rain! We conversed about so many things as I reapplied the makeup I cried off. I walked out from my bathroom to see a small stuffed animal. It had been one month and honestly, I had not done much in that month. But trust me, I had walked from my bedroom to the bathroom often, and I had never seen this stuffed animal before. It startled me.

"Oh my gosh," I said to Rain, "There's this stuffed animal sitting on the chair. Where did this come from?"

Immediately she asked, "Is it Taz?"

"I don't know, it looks like a little bear." I snapped a picture and sent it to her. She tells me, "Yes, that is Taz! I gave that to him when we worked at the zoo!"

She then sent me a picture of two stuffed animals. The Tasmanian devil (Taz) she bought for Josiah, and her own stuffed animal she bought at the same time.

I asked my granddaughter if she had moved it to my room? No.

I asked Jeremy, Valerie and Michael. No. They had not seen it.

Where had it come from? I knew it was Josiah's -- Rain had made that clear. But as you recall, we had taken a stuffed animal to Josiah. I had two stuffed monkeys with me on the drive, Joe being one of them! I am all about the stuffed animals, and I would have known if I had picked up this little one. Richard had not brought it in from the car, none of the kids had picked it up. Nobody knew where it came from. It had just appeared on the one-month anniversary, and while I was on the phone with Rain!

Right after the Tasmanian devil stuffed animal appearance, I received a text message from a friend I have known for years but do not talk to often. When we do, it is usually health-related questions she's asking me. Now, out of the blue she had texted, *your son is worried about you. He wants your rainbow glow around you back! Your glow is gray now!* Of course, it is, everything is gray now! Then she wrote, *Josiah is with you all the time. His spirit left his body before impact. That he walked up and saw his body there.* This was the same thing Kelly had heard him say in her dream and the exact feeling I had around this. He was making sure his signs were unmistakable.

Thanksgiving 2017

Thanksgiving has always been the most important holiday of the year. My father was not so religious, and holidays were far from important to him – except for Thanksgiving. He lit up over this day, and wanted everyone to come feast at his table, and on my mother's cooking. As my mother aged, I took over this tradition. Thanksgiving became the mandatory family gathering, so much so, I do it on the weekend before Thanksgiving to make sure all the family can come. Josiah, my wanderer, knew this well, and would try his best to attend, even if it was his voice being passed around on the phone. My mother had opened the door to eternity on November 18, 2014. Now, three years later, I am headed towards another heart-wrenching Thanksgiving, without the physical presence of my son. How do I enter a day of thanks? How do I cook? How do I eat? It's a mere four weeks from the worst day of my life and I am paralyzed.

I forced myself to leave the house and go to the store, but instead, I drove straight to my daughter's floral shop. Being in her presence gave me a pause from the babbling brook my blood had become. The chaos in my heart. Earlier I had seen on Facebook that a medium, Lillian Suarez, was hosting a free event to anyone who had a child in Spirit. As I sat watching Valerie create her floral boutiques of magic, I remembered it was time for Lillian's talk. I opened my phone to listen to her. She was getting messages and waiting until the recipient identified with what she was saying. Then she would continue reading for them. I said nothing, just listened.

Then Lillian changed the way she was doing the reading. She explained that she was now going to go direct, which means she was going to contact the spirit first, find who she thinks it is for. She began with, "I have a son, he left fast, it was unexpected!!"

Josiah, Josiah! I recited in my mind.

Then her voice said what my ears wanted to hear: "I want to come to Raina. My awareness is being brought to you. Do you have a son in Spirit?"

"Yes!"

"He desperately wants to come in, and he tells me he loves you. I feel like he wants to tell you he is sorry, but he didn't have control, do you understand this?"

I whimper, "Yes!"

"He says, 'I am sorry, Mom. He talks about feeling like something was going to happen, like he wasn't going to be here, do you understand that?"

Yes, I understood this. I knew he was letting me know that this was about way more than just the wreck. All I kept saying was "Yes, yes, yes."

"I didn't want to leave," she continued on Josiah's behalf. "I love you so much. I do not want to see you cry." She paused. "It really hurt him to see you sad. Can you understand that? You were everything to him. He told me he was very close to you. You talk to him often and he hears you. He says, "Thank you for waking up every day and talking to me." He says, "I am learning now, here on the other side." Then she repeated what I had been told, "his soul lifted before he hit."

She went on to describe Josiah, then said, "He communicated well, but he picked and chose who he let in and trusted. He was polite, and he still is. He is giving evidence, stopping, giving evidence, stopping." Lillian then mentioned October and February. I told her that he'd passed in October and February was his sister's birthday. She said, "He has a brother, right?", then, "Gum. Did he chew gum?"

I had to laugh then. "No, I did! All the time, and he picked on me for it."

She said again that he loved me, and that he lived for making me proud. I don't know if I would have believed that, but for an incident that last summer when he was buying a car. He had asked me my opinion about trading his truck in for another car. I told him to wait until he was more established in his job at Apple, which he had just started. But Josiah wanted what he wanted. He did not want to wait. So, he asked me my opinion again, but in a different way. I laughed and gave him my same answer. A few days later he called again and asked in yet another way. Finally, I said, "Son, if you want to buy the car, buy the car, you do not need my approval."

And then he said something I did not remember ever hearing: "I just don't want to disappoint you, Mom!"

I was dumbfounded. "Oh, son, I could never be disappointed in you, why would you even think that?"

"I just want to know you think I am making the right decision!"

"Josiah, baby, it's a car, do what makes you happy!"

Now, when Lillian said that he wanted to make me

proud, I was taken back to that conversation. She told me that we had a closeness, a unique closeness, a soul connection. And that I was wrestling with whether I should have known. Which, of course, was true. But I did know, deep within.

Then she said, "It feels like yesterday, like this just happened yesterday."

I told her it had been a little over a month. It made sense now, she said, about him giving evidence and stopping. That he was doing a really good job for someone who had so recently arrived over there. He told her he was looking out after his sister, and that he was observing what was going on.

He told Lillian, "I'm always around you, Mom," and that he did not want to talk about him being gone, because he was still here. He told her I had done a good job teaching him to be strong, He said he was strong there. He talked about the tree and something we did in memory of a tree. He asked that my heart would be at peace and not to worry because everything was going to be okay. He knew I had his clothes, and I was holding them to be connected to him. That it would get easier. Then Lillian said he wanted me to know that when I see a butterfly, it would be him. I told her the story of the butterfly in the tree, the one that showed us what happened to him. And that butterflies were my thing. That he drew and painted me butterflies. She then described my couch and the exact corner he sat in when he came over.

"He still sits there with you."

That was an unexpected Thanksgiving moment. I

knew when we all gathered, he would be there. I bought him vegan eggnog, our tradition. We toasted his magic.

Sitting on the couch after dinner, my daughter-in-love, also named Valerie, told me she had a dream about Josiah.

The three of us—she, Josiah and I—were sitting together at a table. No words were spoken. She said he was smiling like she knew what he was saying, but there were no words. He was speaking to her through his mind. He was watching us (her and I) as we looked at all his drawings. She said he was full of joy. He was happy that we were looking at his drawings. Then the scene switched and she saw him alone. Smiling. Dark was around him and he was holding a single small white candle. And then he blew it out.

At that time, when his departure was still so new, I could not emotionally process that the candle was blown out. That he was in the dark. It felt so abstract and painful. But now that I write it to you, it makes more sense to me. He was showing her that he was watching us. He saw what we were doing. The candle that he was holding was spiritual enlightenment and blowing it out meant he was blowing out all the negativity, leaving only his smile illuminated!

I went with you

I am asleep. In a dream state that has no rest.

Unable to wake. I toss and turn to the rhythm that has no beat.

I cannot follow the sound, for it is unrecognizable in the silence.

Neither my left, nor my right foot can move to the sudden sounds, I cannot hear, but are deafening.

My body sways motionless. My breath is airless.

My bones bend to accommodate the spontaneous lack of motion.

My heart stops as I stare, then beats as I glance away, and then stops again.

I went with you.

~Raina, December 12, 2017

Christmas 2017

Strong loathing surrounded this holiday that I should have been rejoicing in. The brisk air and the smell of fireplaces burning warmth, into the homes that are illuminated with multicolored lights, and figurines of reindeers, snowmen, and Santa, were dimmed by the hazy eyelids I was looking through. There is still so much here. So much that I love. I could not shake the gloom that had swallowed me. It had only been two months. My broken heart was just a fraction of the size it once was. I paused to think what it must look like – a million tiny embryonic pieces, each one needing its own blood supply so it could grow into some unique direction towards each other, hopefully reassembling into a shape that I would recognize. I just wanted my son. I wanted him to once more surprise me and knock on the door.

"Fooled you, Mom. I was just away in the Himalayan mountains. I was at a monastery. I had taken a vow of silence; I didn't mean to worry you."

I continued to daydream. Begging for this to be true. Telling him, "I just want to hear from you." Shifting from that begging, to normal conversation, to begging again. "I am going to give Valerie the flute that you two picked out together. I know she wants it. Jeremy wants it too!"

I had brought home several flutes from Josiah's, which he had on consignment to sell, to return to John the Flute maker. Over the last two months, I had watched Jeremy go over to the flutes and play them. Connecting to his brother in song. I knew I had to keep one of these for Jeremy too. Within that thought I got up to call John and arranged to meet with him, I just needed one more watch with Jeremy. Jeremy came over and just as predicted, he and his sons went to play the flutes. I asked him, "Which is your favorite?" He played each one. I could see he was curious himself as to which one he would favor.

"This one!" he said finally, holding it up. I nonchalantly said, "Oh cool," and said no more.

After the flute exchange with John was made, it became clear to me that Josiah had something to say to his siblings. I sat down and within minutes, Josiah had written to his brother through my pen. I was sobbing, and in truth, somewhat astonished. I read it and read it and read it. Each time crying harder than the read before.

"Son, this is so beautiful... How did I? Thank You!" This was new. I had written to Jeremy from Josiah! I had channeled him! Through setting my intention, meditation and automatic writing, the practice of writing words from the unconscious mind, his words began to flow. I wanted to dance, scream, cry, laugh and tell everyone. But I could not. It was not Christmas yet, and he still had something to say to his sister. Again, I put my pen to paper, and his voice danced across the tear-stained pages. Suddenly I could not wait for Christmas. He had knocked on the door of my spirit and surprised me. He was here gifting his brother and sister with flutes, and songs that would be with them for the rest of their lives. And I was hearing him, loud and clear.

We were giving the grandkids bows and arrows for Christmas. Jeremy was clueless one of these boxes held his flute. Some Christmases are held over multiple days in my giant family. Valerie could not come to the first evening gathering, but I could not wait another minute to give Jeremy this letter and his flute. I handed him a blue folder with the words of Josiah, then the house grew quiet as we all witnessed the heart of my firstborn child meld with his brother's.

Jeremy,

From the minute I was born I looked up to you, my big brother, the one who was going to lead the way.

I watched you and then I did what you did.

As we grew older, I could see we were different yet the same. Our hands were instruments of creativity, our Spirits adventurous and our hearts wide open to take in love and give it freely.

Though I traveled a different path than you, it was always parallel to yours, and when our paths crossed, you were always there for me, seeing my vision and helping me to create it.

We still have more creativity to do.

You are a Master Builder, use your gifts, create and now it will be I, that walks beside you, seeing your visions and guiding you.

Just think of me and I will be there,

Brother to Brother

Heart to Heart

Builder to Builder

Artist to Artist

Imagine it, then create, it's the best surprise when you blow your own self away.

Take care of Mom---You give her Strength

Life is love

Love is Healing

Healing is Peace

I am in the sounds of silence and the music that fills your heart with Me.

Play Me often.

Josiah

He looked up at me with tears – "Mom?" – then he thanked me and reached out to hug me. I handed him the box. His eyes welled deeper. He knew. The magic on his face, and the light in his eyes, as he played his flute will linger inside my soul forever. We gathered again the next evening. It was hard for me to contain myself. I handed Valerie her blue folder and hushed the house. She already had her brother's flute. She had taken it home with her from our time in Santa Cruz. It was the last thing she had done with her brother and I knew she was silently praying I would never ask her for it. I did not think she was going to make it through the letter, but she did.

Sister, Valerie, Friend,

We shared something really special, connected through a lineage of time and space. It was obvious, the way we created games that only the two of us could play, and the way we sought other, sibling friends, so we could stay together...

We shared a belief that it is better to be our own unique self than follow the norm...

I always trusted you, I trust you now, for you only allow Beauty to filter in, guarding Love and the hearts you love...

Thank you, time and time again I should have thanked you but I didn't, so I am thanking you now, for allowing yourself to evolve, for listening to your Spirit and triumphing, for never allowing what could have stopped you to stump you, for leaving, for learning, for loving...

There was so much we were going through together,

different fears, yet fear is fear...

different challenges, yet a challenge is a challenge...

different pain, yet pain is pain...

Together we walked on thorns and together we walked on water...

I am so proud of You – I see You – I have always seen you – so I would fill my jewels with my energy and my love and pass them to you –

My only Sister...

There is an unseen magic that you see now,

An unheard song you hear now,

And an unknown knowing you know now,

Love is an unmistakable force that has no beginning and no end,

Beautiful, Healing and Powerful,

Our Bond is eternal, ethereal, enlightened and encrypted...

I am here, I haven't gone away,

When your heart is low, I am there,

when your heart is full, I'm there,

A dust storm – Me

The soft sound of rain, a light flickering, chocolate,

And the unique need to laugh... Me...

It's me When you think of carbies and barbies,

Prescott, health food and the multiple ways to reduce stress...

A feather, a penny, a dime...

And Valerie, when the wind whistles a melody of its own,

It's me,

playing my flute for you...

And only you,

I Love You

Josiah

Valerie looked up at me, completely bewildered, and said, "How is this possible?" What a perfect question to such a mysterious letter. As we hugged and cried, I said, "I don't know, it just is!" She looked back down at the letter, and then at me. Tears streamed from her eyes. Her relief mixed with pain and joy that this flute that they shared in picking out, they would be sharing for the rest of her life too.

This was, and might forever be, the greatest gift I have ever given my children, and myself. I had found a secret within myself. I could channel Josiah. He had come home, found a way to bridge the distance between us.

"I didn't mean to worry you, Mom; I am so sorry."

"I know, son, I just miss you so much, this is going to take me a lifetime to process!"

"I know Mom, I will be with you every step of the way, I promise. I am standing right next to you!"

December 29, 2017
Dream

I was at a show where they parade the ones we love in Spirit. Several of us were sitting in the bleachers, waiting to see Josiah, but that is vague. There were a lot of Spirits, all of them taking turns talking to their family in the audience. I grew so tired of waiting, I fell asleep, and when I woke up, I thought I might have missed Josiah. But then he came in, a little boy of six or seven, with a group of other kids. His face was scratched like what might have been the result of the accident, though the actual accident had not left any marks on his face. I could see the rash from his being ill that summer. Still, he was being silly with the other kids. Playful, just like Josiah would be here in this life. I was so happy to see him. Then the scene changed. I was where they lived, it felt like a small hotel, or a bed and breakfast. I was in a lobby sitting on a chair by the front desk. I called him and he walked over to me and sat on my lap. I told him I loved him. I hugged him and said everyone loved him and that I missed him. I kept hugging and kissing him and looking at his face. He was so young. He seemed to be wondering. I told my friend Kim to take a picture as I was holding him and loving on him. She took a distant picture, and I can remember the feeling of me wanting her to come closer and take more.

This dream had me stumped. I had channeled such beautiful words just a few days prior. Why was I seeing this image, and did it have meaning? Was this a visitation? I decided to do what I had done before. Write. I asked for clarity since I was a bit disturbed by it. "Josiah was this you or just my subconscious mind seeping in during the night?"

"Mom, do you see? You can come and see me! We are all waiting to talk with you! We line up waiting for the ones we love to communicate with us! You see me young, because I am new here, and that was a time you are fond of. You see my scars, my wounds and you know my fears and insecurities. I could not hide them from you. I know you love me, and I love you; Did you see me laughing in line? Everything is new. I feel like a kid again! I know you miss me."

This made sense to me, even though my images were so intense. I really shouldn't have been surprised; my dreams can really take me on a journey! Unbeknownst to me, my dream journey had only begun.

January 8, 2018
A Clearing with Shaman Isabella

The kindness of my sweet strong friend was moving; her words have strength and are deliberate. Her intention was to clear away blockages in me and in Josiah, freeing us both to move through the ethers with grace. Ascend to our next level with clarity of purpose. To embrace the value that this pain will bring me. It sounds so far removed that I could assign value to a heartbreak this grand. And will I? Will I be fully present with all the emotions that come up as a result of Josiah going to Spirit? Will I be able to see this as part of his mission? That he would leave at a specific time, and be like a magnet that instigates in my heart a depth of healing that could *only* be healed by this kind of tragedy?

Will I embrace a new depth of understanding that only heartbreak allows one to get to? Will I do the unthinkable and grow? Is his journey, his rebirth into the cosmos, also mine? We all walk alongside each other. An unrecognized image of ourselves. Will I reflect to you love, and faith, and strength? Will I resolve to be? And will I allow peace to come back, and reign Her mercy once again? Will I be more authentic? More available? A channel for you to come to, to begin your own healing?

With all these questions dangling in my mind, a quote someone once told me dropped in.

It is only by finding safety in the darkness, do we help the darkness remember that it must be the light!

Dream Class

It is now 2018. This reality I am living is trickling by. Why do I get to ring in the new year and Josiah does not? How is this even fair? I feel off balance. What am I supposed to do now? I opened my email one day in early January and found an invitation to a short dream class at our local university. I had taken this class before and enjoyed it. With the dreams that were now coming in, I thought this might be the kind of therapy I needed. Eight total strangers would soon walk with me through an entrance only I would see, but they would know they had a hand in it!

First Dream in the Class

I woke up in the middle of the night with this knowing I was to use a certain essential oil. I just could not recall the oil, only the emotion of it, *community*. I repeated community over and over in my head, knowing how the night's mind tends to forget. I finally got up and wrote it down on the first thing I saw, a grocery receipt. *Community*. In the morning I looked up the oil of community and it was cedarwood. Cedarwood is earthy and grounding. Of course, it's a tree oil. Cedarwood blends the emotions of the heart chakra to stabilize the root chakra. I was definitely not grounded and in fact had just said, "I don't feel balanced!"

I continued to read about cedarwood and how it helps with feelings of disconnection, isolation and opens the heart to receive love and support. It opens the eye to see that you are not alone, that life is a shared experience. Confirmation I was in the right class for me? Or just a bizarre coincidence? Since I don't believe in coincidence, only kismet, I knew this was a powerful message from Josiah. As I closed my eyes and pressed my pen against the paper, I could hear him:

"Mom you're not alone, everything you and I have gone through is for a realization, and we will go through the rest of this experience together. This is our shared experience, and because of all the people we love, we have to go on. Be the experience, Mom. Live the experience. Experience the experience and give love in the experience. Mom, receive the love in this experience. Connect your heart to the roots of your feet – be cedarwood!"

"Wow! Okay, son, I understand. You are happy I am peeking around the tree I had been hiding behind..."

Would I continue to hide? A little, but I was peeking, and it felt good to be in community, even if it was only one day a week. We met every Wednesday for six weeks. Every week there would be new shifts and realizations for all of us. On the last day of the class I asked if I could read what I had written about Josiah at his Celebration of Life. "Yes!" they all said, "We feel as if we know him through all you have shared."

The following week I gathered photos of Josiah to share with them, as well as my writing. When I went to class, I normally walked on the left of the building to get around it and into the front door, but on this day the parking I found led me around the right side. This side was more treed and closer to the street. I accidentally dropped my journal, and as I knelt to pick it up, there were several orange and gray feathers laying on the ground. I never pass up a feather, or several for that matter, for they are signs from the angels and the ones we love in Spirit. I examined them. They looked foreign, like I had never seen feathers like these. As I picked them all up and rushed to the meditation room where we were holding class, I thought about the colors. Orange, I knew, symbolizes creativity, intuition and emotions. Grey is neutral and a sign of inner peace. Exactly what Josiah would want for me and what this class had done for all of us. We had all been so deeply touched by each other's lives and dreams.

I waited to be the last to share. I knew it was going to be rough. I read my tribute to these beautiful women who had graciously held my heart for six weeks, each one crying and telling me how they felt like they had known Josiah his whole life. I pulled out the feathers and told them how I had found them on the way in. Hoping I had enough, I laid an orange and gray feather in front of each of them, thanking them for sharing their hearts with mine. When I was done passing out the feathers, we all sat in amazement as I held the last feather in my hand. Without knowing, I had been given the exact number of feathers for myself and my classmates. Was it I, thanking them? Or was he?

I Love You More Tattoos

Jaye met Josiah in that chrysalis time, back when he ventured to Joshua Tree, but for other reasons. She, the tattoo queen of the desert, would be the one to adorn his body with symbols of the chakras, feathers, oms and hertz vibrations. On that last trip to Joshua Tree, when we visited John the Flute maker and Valerie helped Josiah pick out the flute, we also visited Jaye. It was a pleasant surprise for all of us. Josiah had adorned her shop, with wooden wonders and elfin benches. They had a deep bond and clear connection. As we were all visiting, an unfamiliar man walked into the shop. Jaye describes him as an older punk rocker-looking guy. He asked Jaye if he could have a pencil and paper and draw. Jaye obliged him. He then sat down in the waiting area, quietly drawing. We all continued our con-versations, and when we left the man was still there. This quiet artist handed Jaye what he had drawn and left. Jaye has never seen him since. She looked at the drawing and thought, "Wow!" and put it on the front desk and went on with her busy day of tattooing.

Two years prior, on Mother's Day, I thought Josiah had neglected to call me. He was, as usual, out of the state. I spent the day with his siblings, waiting and somewhat miffed! "How could he forget? Yet why would he remember? He was frolicking!"

I waved through my mind, allowing my heart to be okay if he had forgotten. As the orange and pink rays of sunset were setting the evening sky, I heard his text. Relieved, I sprinted to my phone, where the words "I didn't forget you!" sailed into my heart. His words might have been delayed until the end of the day, but what he gave me was more than a present. There in my message was a picture. Josiah's eyebrows raised to express his reasons for delay. His arm across the screen. He had been tattooed that day, with the words, *I love you more* (in Hebrew!) This was my dream, to have "I love you more" tattooed on myself with my children. The idea had been brewing for a year or so, and obviously Josiah was tired of waiting. He wanted me to know how deep his love was for me. Within that picture was everything my son could have ever said to me. Now I wanted this tattoo more than ever!

Jaye came to his Celebration of Life. She made sure Jeremy, Valerie and I were together when she told us that instead of flowers, she would like to gift the family a tattoo!

Immediately Jeremy said, "I love you more!"

"Yes! Yes!" Valerie and I harmonized, as grateful tears strayed from our eyes and a silent energy swept around us. *Josiah's*, for sure.

I was thinking to myself whether we were all going to get it in black, just like Josiah's, when Jeremy said, "I want mine in camo colors!" That question had been answered, but what did I want?

"Who's going first?" Jaye asked when we got to Jaye's shop that day. In unison, Jeremy and I said, "Valerie!" She's my most tattooed child, although Josiah was a close second. Valerie's arms had no room for our "motto," so she decided it would go along her shoulder.

"What color?" Jaye asked.

Valerie answered her question with a question. "What do you think?"

Jaye then spoke as if Josiah were within her: "The colors of the chakras!"

A light went on in me. "Yes, exactly. That is exactly what I want too!" I left that day so happy, my dream fulfilled! My daughter and I had matching colors, and Jeremy and I had ours placed in the exact same spot on our arms that Josiah's had been.

Six days later, Josiah would thank Jaye. She was going through some papers that had been tucked away on her desk when a random drawing caught her attention. It was Josiah, drawn by the unfamiliar punk rock dude! That man had just sat there, drawing, and of all the things, people or places he could have drawn, he drew Josiah, and listened in enough to our conversation to recognize the name of who he drew. There is no way to deny the vibration Josiah was walking in. From the higher dimension he knew one day he would be thanking Jaye for completing what not only I wanted, but he wanted too, that we all were tattooed together.

Journaling

I had only written a little in the months since this world had scorned me. I had channeled Josiah for his siblings and some powerful words for myself. I had written these intense dreams that I was continuously having. Analyzing them and making sense of my dream world.

One morning while checking my email, which most of the time went unread these days. I noticed an email from Sunny Dawn Johnston. Sunny is an incredible thought-provoking spiritual teacher, mentor, and friend. She was having an online journaling class. Perfect I thought! I could stay in the safety of my withdrawn world, and yet have the guidance I need right now, from my dear friend and teacher. I knew that when I journal and write my feelings and thoughts it helped me. Even if I have no idea what I am writing, even if it is minutiae. Getting it out of my head and on paper, clearing the cobwebs of my mind from the chatter and torture I was allowing to dialogue, would help me gain perspective and open me to be closer to Josiah. I could take on writing for myself, I thought, but I kept the, "I do not have to talk to anyone if I do not want to, since it is online," concept. I quickly learned I did have much to say, in a withdrawn manner, of course. I did not want to expose my brokenness to strangers. But when I introduced myself, I poured out my soul to them. This is my truth, and the process I am in. I was not looking for sympathy, I had purposely stayed off social media for that reason.

I had two local friends that were going through the same thing I was. We were a year or so apart in this journey. Their friendship was, and is, priceless to me.

The moments I got with them left me feeling less crazy. Supported in a way no one else could possibly relate to. I had not thought of venturing out past Sharon and Barbara. But hidden behind my laptop screen, inside my journaling group, and within my post, was something I did not realize I needed: mothers!

Within that post, I met other mothers with children in Spirit. My words were understood and greeted with a vibration of love that was unbreakable. We all quickly made sure each of us stayed connected. Linked together, a chain began, formed with the charms of our children adorning it.

Had I not continued to journal these dreams and thoughts, I might have missed out on the messages that were coming in so quickly. If you have not journaled yet, I highly recommend it, even if you just jot down bullet points to your thoughts and feelings and dreams. When you are ready to dive in, those bullet points will jog your memory and you will be able to start from there. Trust me on this. So many of the stories you've read here started out as bullet points. I promise.

March 11, 2018

Huge day. My house was full of children for my Angel face of love, my granddaughter Skylinn's birthday. After the party, I dropped into Facebook and saw a post from a friend of Josiah's. This was not the first post I'd read that brought me to my knees. There had been so many posts and private messages. Yet six months had passed, and the posts had slowed down. Speechless and breathless, I read it.

The Prophet

Josiah. Our very own Prophet sent to use in some form of mercy, trying to teach the rest of us scoundrels to be More. There are those people you meet that have an aura about them, that makes them stand out and makes you question where they came from. I remember feeling shame the first time I met him. I was not going to be enough for this person to give me the time of day, which is hilarious to think about someone touched by divinity. He was not without his troubles. This world is confusing for those not from it, and I would try and offer as much counsel as I could in my antihero sort of way. I cannot help but feel the relationship being a bit lopsided, I think I got so much more from him than he did from me. I suspect I am not the only person who feels this way, so I let go of such thoughts when I can. I still feel numb to his absence, almost like nothing has happened. How much of me is a monster for not feeling more like everyone else? I imagine it is my mind's way of protecting me from a complete meltdown and this tragedy will take years to unpack. I am dumbfounded as to the impact one soul can make on so many people. Perhaps it is because he died young, but we have all been to funerals where you felt the person's life did almost nothing for anyone. A dim light that passed on no other flames. Josiah, on the other hand, had three services that were packed with beautiful women crying, sages broken and family so strong it was inconceivable. He burned so bright and so hot that darkness itself had to squint. That is how you are supposed to live. That is the message I am left with. Be somebody so amazing that when you die it rocks a coastline. I already miss butting heads with you. I miss your laugh. I do not think I will ever get over this... I do not know if I want to... Whatever plain you are diving in, I hope I will get to hug you again. And from the bottom of my imperfect heart, Thank You. ~ Michael Boeri

"He burned so bright and so hot that darkness itself had to squint!" I must have read Michael's post a hundred times. Each time these words sunk deeper and deeper into my soul. Awed by the inspired life Josiah led. He touched a span of humanity. He lived like he was on a quest to accomplish all he could. Like he knew that his time on earth was short, though he certainly did not want to leave.

In my need to find sense in the senseless, Michael Boeri pulled back a curtain of my tattered soul and let some light in.

March 17, 2018: Path Dream

The dream class had ended but my dreams would not. Shortly after my last class, I had another dream. I do love the crisp clarity of my dreams, but this one was vague. What I do remember is Josiah brought his father to my dream state. He walked into my house with him. I could feel Mitchell's sadness. There were others at my house – most likely, the kids and grandkids – but it was his father I could feel.

I woke from that dream, wrote it down and fell back asleep. And had another dream. This one so intense and profound I can remember it with that crisp clarity.

I dreamt I was taking Josiah to a birthday party. In

my dream, I had just been with his older brother Jeremy as an adult. (At the time, I was keeping Jeremy's five-year-old son, Gavin, with me instead of him going to school, but Gavin was Josiah. So, Josiah showed up as Gavin in my dream. This is something that would continue in several dreams to come.) The day of the birthday party he was wearing lighter color shorts and a white tank top with stripes. I remember feeling like he was not really dressed for the party, but this is what he had on! I felt like we were supposed to go somewhere else after this party. Like we were ditching school, going to this party and then somewhere else. Like Disneyland! When we got to the party, there were a lot of kids there, and they were in every room. Upstairs. Downstairs. The family room, living room and kitchen. Josiah decided he wanted to go into the living room. I was in the doorway between the kitchen and the living room watching him. Josiah walked about halfway into the living room when all of a sudden, a mist came, like fog, and I lost view of him. I went immediately after him shouting his name. "Josiah, where are you? Josiah!" The rest of the dream I was searching for him. No other parent at this party would help me. They were more concerned about what they were doing, no matter how I told them he was missing! They showed no concern. It was like I was invisible. I went in every room, so worried that someone had stolen him and at the same time puzzled how this could happen. Where was this mist from? How did this happen right before my eyes? I kept searching. No child could hear me or respond. Then the scene changed. I was now outside on top of a hill. I saw a man in the distance down below this hill with many dogs. Big dogs, possibly shepherds. The man was playing music on a stringed instrument. He looked like an older version of Josiah, but I could not sense if it is him. Suddenly, I was in a seated position with my legs straight out and I was sliding towards this man down the hill. My legs landed on top of his legs. I told him what is going on and asked, would he come and help me find Josiah? I told him this must be why we met! He came with me to the house. Now I was tearing everything apart! I was looking in the cabinets, in the drawers, in the closets. Upstairs. Downstairs. Frantically tearing everything apart. In the meantime, the man had finally found the father of the child who was having the party and was speaking to him. The owner of the house had no idea where Josiah was. I walked up to the owner and said, "If he is not here, where is the next place I should look?" He walked me to the front door and pointed. There at the front door was a long path that led to picturesque hills. Maybe the hill I was just on, where I'd met the man playing music? To the left of the path was the city with some trees. To the right was a meadow and mountains. The path itself was very wide with nothing on it. Not a pebble. It was straight. It was smooth. It was long, but not too long, two or three miles that led directly to the hills, where I sensed a creek or river was.

I was shaken out of this dream by my husband, because I was making a lot of noise and crying. I composed myself, told Rich everything, and jumped out of bed to write it down. As terrifying as the dream was, it was true. The fact that I thought Josiah was not wearing appropriate clothes made perfect sense. He was wearing motorcycle gear, not his elfin bohemian clothes, when he left! He had vanished right before my eyes and

I was looking in every nook and cranny for him. I was reading every book I could get. Furthering my studies in mediumship and anything else to help me understand the afterlife. And just like the parents and children in the dream could not see what I was doing or help me, no one could grasp what I was doing. This was mine to unravel. Was this mysterious music man with shepherds, my shepherd? Was this that Spirit guide I'd been told was coming? The one I told Jeanette about when the butterfly showed up? He had come with me to search for Josiah. He was the one who found the owner. He was the one who got them to pay attention. That party was chaos. Just like my mind had been, but just outside the door of my mind, the owner, or "The Ethereal," was showing me that my journey was easier than I was making it. Yes, it would be a long path, but not so long I could not walk it. It was smooth, with no rocks to trip me up. It showed me each side of my path. To the left where the city was, is my life on earth. To the right is my spiritual life. If I stayed in the middle, I could manage both, and be led straight down that path and find exactly what I am looking for. Josiah.

March 22, 2018: Five Months

I sit blank, aimless, everything without form. You are the first thing I think of as I arise out of bed. I speak your name to breathe you back to me. Immediately I am filled with anticipation that today, again, we will connect. Stronger and more tangible than the day before. I feel my cheek quiver. You are kissing me. I feel you touching the top of my head as if you are grabbing my hair like when you were young. I pull a card because the energy is so intense, and I know you have something to say. Once again, the cards remind me, "We *are so connected*," and "You *will always point me in the right direction!*" I am just wondering where that direction could be, without you here on earth with me. My mind begins to wrestle with my guilt. I should have done more. Why did I not say more, do more, be more? You tell me it was not my fault over and over, through these cards and through people. But how do I not hold some former responsibility for your health? Your decisions? You are my son! How, I ask, how? How do I set aside responsibility and trust the process of life?? Tell me what to do, Josiah?

And just like that, I am writing!

Hold fast, Mom, I am with you. Trust the elements. Trust the world you see. Trust the sensations in your body. Trust your dreams. Trust the complexity of life and trust our bond, I am asking you to trust the Universe in its beautiful collaboration with me. We got you. All those secret surprises I wanted to do, the times you thought I forgot, I did not. I never forgot the grace in which you performed. The diligence in your manner. The dance you danced to keep me happy and calm. The money you spent, and the time you sacrificed. I am the one who wanted to do more for you. I am the one who is sorry. Be at peace, Mom, I am with you. I have always been with you. Generations upon generations. Time and time again. This time I came in as your son. Recall the memory of me being your father also. We are the same. We will always be the same. Can you feel me? Feel me, Mom. I am here, leaving you signs, messages, and direction. Hear me,

Mom. Listen to the wind and the inner wisdom of your soul. That too, is me. See me, Mom, I am in everything you do. Have no doubt. Have absolutely no doubt. I am here, with you always and forever. I love you more. Josiah

April 6, 2018

This dream was rough.

A friend was driving and I was the passenger in her car. We were on the way home from a concert. It was just the two of us. We had something with us that we thought might be illegal, but also knew that it was not illegal, so we knew we had no reason to be spooked. We were coming over the border from one state to another and they were doing a police search. They waved us over to the side. My friend was in the driver seat and I am now in the passenger side back seat. The policeman is sitting backwards towards me in the front passenger seat. Then he gets in the back and moves the front seat forward and is facing me. I tell him since there is nothing for you to arrest me for, I am going to get out of the car now. I lean to get out, but he is huge. I realize he is not moving, and he is not really a police officer. I look towards my left. There is a couple there now. I do not know where they came from. They were towards the front seat, but there was no seat. We are all in the back. The couple is moving towards me as they are going to embrace me with their energy. I push them back towards each other so they can just embrace each other. Right over the top of them I see the man who had been blocking my way out. He is on the other side of them. I realized I am not getting out of this.

There is no way out. I feared what was next! Was I going to be raped or murdered? There was no escape! I began to cry.

Rich woke me up. I was crying for real and continued to cry for about an hour. This dream really got to me. When I finally gained back my calm, I could see what the dream represented. The concert and the things we thought were illegal, being in the car with a friend, all represented escape. I desperately wanted to escape this pain! The police were protection, of which there is none. No matter what I do, or where I go, or who I am with, there is no escaping this. There is a part of me that is not in the driver seat. Not behind the wheel of my life. I am a passenger. Pushed to the backseat by what feels like, powerful energies trying to consume me. And the emotionless huge person not allowing me out of the car? That is grief blocking the door and peering over me. Whatever I do, I cannot push it away. The feeling I am about to be raped or murdered? That is the feeling of having a part of myself ripped away, feeling that I must live in this consumption.

April 07, 2018

The very next night I have this dream.

I went to the eye doctor. The doctor told me my eyes were better. I did not need such a strong prescription anymore. I sat with the eye doctor chatting, as if we were old friends. We talked about our dads dying when we were young, and the pain it caused us. I told her about Josiah. We both sat there, crying. She had to leave and forgot to give me my prescription for my new glasses. The receptionist scrambled to get a hold of the doctor to get it for me. When I left the doctor's office, I felt daring. My car was parked on a steep road. It was a muscle car. I got in the car and peeled out across a huge intersection that led me to an eight-lane highway, through picturesque mountains with colors I had never seen before. Magical, like you would see deep in the ocean. I knew I was in another state, not California. I was enchanted and exhilarated as I cruised down the highway.

What this dream showed me is my vision was clearer. The previous night's dream had helped me recognize how I was crippling myself emotionally. This dream was showing me that I could move through that. I was ready to take on life. I was still going to scramble to find my clarity but that was okay. I could still dare something new. I do have strength, like that muscle car. The roads were wide. The mountains were colorful. I was ready and capable of seeing everything more vividly.

These dreams also showed me how quickly we can transmute our own energy by just recognizing what is going on. I could have let my dream scare me, but deep within, I knew better. I knew this was me, talking to myself in my dream.

Rosemary and Juniper Berry Essential Oil Experience

It was just one of those days. I knew I needed to process through something because all I could do was mope. I looked to my essential oils to help me work through something, anything! Plant medicine vibrates to its own rhythm and I needed the music they could provide. I put

Rosemary on my neck for grief, and Juniper Berry on my heart for fear. Within minutes I was crying uncontrollably. Sobbing in my grief. Laying on the floor in a puddle. After quite a cry, I came into my healing room. I pulled out the Talking to Heaven deck. I was just holding them. I felt so broken. I finally began to shuffle them, waiting for a card to fly out.

First card to fly: *"You have nothing to feel guilty about."*

I spoke out loud, crying. "Josiah I wasn't ready, I wasn't ready. I was never going to be ready."

Second card: *"I'm so sorry, please forgive me."*

I continued to cry, saying, "I don't know what to do. I don't know what to do!

Third card: *"I will always point you in the right direction."* Blown away. He was answering me! I continued to speak to him out loud. I asked, "Where do I go? I do not want to go anywhere without you. I just want you to call me! I just want to be with you!"

Fourth card: *"We will be together again!"* I lost it! I had just had a conversation with my son!

Gail

Josiah never misses an opportunity to show me how amplified our connection is. This time he was going to take me to a whole new level of understanding. Gail became a second mother energy to Josiah early in his healing journey, when he learned the benefits of hydro-colon therapy. He sought out Gail's wisdom and healing touch. Gail was smitten by my son's brilliant light, and was available to him, and for him, any time he reached out to her. And of course, in true Josiah manner, he insisted we meet. My bond to Gail was kindred mother, there to heal Josiah.

As April crept in, I felt an intense urge to call Gail. This would be our first conversation since Josiah left. I was honored when she immediately answered. We began to share tales of Josiah through the phone. I felt her warm arms hug my soul, and then she asked me, "Did Josiah ever tell you I am a psychic?" I paused, baffled. Memories of conversations about Gail flooded my mind, but I could not recall him ever saying that she was a psychic.

"He told me you did reiki during your therapies, but I don't think he ever told me that!"

Her next words mystified and comforted me. "First, I see you writing a book, what it's like as a spiritual mother to lose a spiritual child!"

"I have always wanted to write a book," I said quietly, "but not about this!"

"It would be amazing!" Then, she floored me. "Josiah wants you to know that, He knew you would not and could not let him go! You would have done anything you could for him! He wants you to know he ascended! My body felt nothing. There was no fear. My soul left before impact. I ascended; I chose my time. I chose this, Mom. I could not do this to you anymore. But I am still here!"

"Ascended!" I weepily whispered. *"He ascended!"* How did I miss that word! "I've been searching for a word that could flow out of my mouth for months! He passed, crossed, left, are some of the words I use, but they never felt right, and I certainly would not say died! I just can't say that, Gail!"

"Because there is no death, Raina!"

"I know, I know, ascended!"

She had confirmed what I have known all along. I *had* seen the magnificence, the divinity of Josiah's choice from where he wanted me to see it. My boy did see the portal. He left, and the motorcycle followed. I hung up the phone in awe and quickly grabbed my journal to write everything we had spoken of. As soon as I finished writing, I was quickened to let four cards leap from the Talking to Heaven deck. Why four, I don't know, I just do what I think I am supposed to do. I have stopped questioning it. If I thought I was in awe before, Josiah would take me to the next level. There before me was exactly what Gail had told me.

Card 1: "I had to leave this way!"

Card 2: "I am not dead!"

Card 3: "There is no death!"

Card 4: "I feel healthy and happy!"

I sat on the floor, awestruck, as tears and snot cascaded their way to the floor. "Josiah," I cried, and I cried, and I cried. *"Compose yourself, Mom, write Gail!"* Though it felt like hours, this all happened within five minutes of our phone conversation. I took a picture of the cards and wrote Gail. "So, immediately after we hung up I wrote what you said to me. Then I sat down on the floor and picked these cards."

"OMG!!!! He speaks VERY CLEARLY!!!!! Amazing!!!"

she replied, then added, "But then that was Josiah!"

"I literally fell backwards in tears," I wrote, "He is almost scolding me, LOL, this is happening constantly, I will dream. Write it down and pull some cards and he just speaks. But today was a mind-blower for sure!"

"Presents from Josiah." she replied with claps and hearts that flooded my screen, "Keep them coming baby, keep them coming" I prayed as I knelt once more in adoration of the bond he and I share.

Apr 22, 2018
Isabella's Earth Day Fire Ceremony

I am now at the sixth month anniversary of Josiah's ascension, but it still feels like I am at day one. I have dreamt so much, and had so many profound experiences, and yet I cannot seem to dry out. I have no idea what to do with myself, at what seems like such a crucial moment in time. Then I saw Isabella was having a fire ceremony at her healing center in Orange County. I wrote just to tell her about the timing of the ceremony, and she replied, asking me to come down and spend the night. She could tell I was hesitant to drive the hour or so in both directions, but I forced myself to do it. I knew it would be good for me.

I had no idea I would have to speak. A speaking stick was being passed as each person told their story, or their intention, or why they were there. The closer it came to my turn, the more my heart was welling up from my eyes. My mind was trying to streamline information. I looked to see the stick was now in my hand.

Crap! It was my turn, but no words were forming. I looked at Isabella for permission to just pass the stick. "I can't do this!" I telepathically told her. She replies out loud. "Yes, you can! You got this. You are with your tribe!" I was with my tribe of like-minded people, but I didn't know anyone except Isabella!

Through snot and tears I forged through. Not sure if what I was saying was recognizable to the ears of my listeners. I told them my heart is shattered, that this is six months since my youngest child ascended. Fluids, without reprieve, fell from my unrecognizable face. Why wouldn't she just let me pass the speaking stick?! I was in no shape to speak, but it was a must. This was my truth. This unimaginable truth. The horror I was speaking fell out of my mouth to the earth, mama earth, the only woman who could absorb these tears and use them as nourishment. Exactly what Josiah would have asked of my tears. I ended my anguish with a glance back to Isabella. I saw her heart beating in her eyes. I could feel everyone's arms around me, yet no one moved. Not a word was spoken until I passed the stick and the next person spoke their truth.

After everyone had said their talking stick message and the ceremony was over, we had a break before meditation. Immediately I was approached by a young woman. She told me she went to massage school with Josiah. Of course, she did! I was an hour and a half from my house, in the middle of Orange County, at an event I had never been to before, and a stranger to me was now a sister, because of Josiah. Another validation of his magic. After meditation, another woman, Lucinda, hugged me. An instant bond was received. She was another mother who had nourished the earth with her tears. She wrapped me up in her heart and cradled me in her words, with the nourishment of knowing, I was not alone.

Patricia

I met Patricia at the Fire ceremony at Isabella's. We chatted and realized she lived in the mountains near me, and decided that we would get together. She wanted me to drive up and do a shamanic ceremony with her on behalf of Josiah. I agreed. I love our local mountains and knew this was important to do. I had not traveled the mountain roads since I had been up in the Santa Cruz mountains where Josiah left. I was a bit panicked. I did not know if I could handle the mountain roads. I knew I had to be dealing with some form of post-traumatic stress, and this could surely trigger me. I did not know what would happen. I almost cancelled on her. I was letting fear get the best of me. I had to con-quer this. Now, our local mountains do not look anything like the mountains up North. But a winding road is a winding road. I decided I was going to embrace this mountain and the curves were going to make me that much stronger.

I put on the song I had sang to him, *In Dreams*. I told myself, "I'm going to embrace this! I am going to take it in. I'm going to play his song, sing it loud and feel it! I'm going to inhale this mountain and when I get to the top, I'm going to exhale the fear!" I turned the music on loud and began singing to him. The turns, the twists of the mountain and the turns and twists in my heart blending together. I finally had to pull over and finish the song parked. I started the car back up, no music, just reflection and embraced the mountain. Patricia took me on a spiritual quest! We ended up out in the hills where we made a ring with pinecones and stones. I had brought pictures of Josiah that I put in the circle. She began playing her drum and I read to her the Tribute of Life I had written for him. She listened, and gently played her drum. A small white butterfly flew in the middle of the circle, then, circled the circle, and flew away. She looked at me and smiled. She knew it was him also. Clearly, I heard him say, *"Mom, you don't need to do this anymore."* From the depth of my being, I knew I had done something to completion.

Mother's Day

Six months disappeared, and Mother's Day came with a vengeance. Oh, Mother's Day. How I love and loathe you. Being a mother is the greatest gift I have been given. I was now an altered form of that sandwiched cookie. The dark icing in between my mother's absence, and now my sons...

The "I love you more" tattoo seemed to create a synergy within me. I knew I needed something to balance this Mother's Day vibe that was brewing within me. And it was still two months away.

Before I joined the tattoo revolution in my fifties, I had told Josiah, "If I ever get a tattoo, it would be a butterfly, with the words, beauty, strength, healing, music, and poetry in it. With a music cord through it, and symbols, representing all my children and grand-children in the cords!" It was just a small talk conversation.

Ten minutes later, Josiah handed me a picture he had quickly sketched for me. "Like this?" he proudly asked as I fixed my eyes upon his creation. He was all about his momma getting a tattoo!

"Yes, this is exactly what I am thinking, but better!"

That was 2011. When I did decide to get a tattoo, it was Mother's Day, 2015, after my mother crossed in November of 2014. My daughter and I wanted to seal her, and our bond, with a mother-daughter tattoo. Still a butterfly, but not the drawing of Josiah's. That was my seal. Valerie and I had our own. After he left this earth, I framed the butterfly drawing, but needed more.

It was a rough draft, but I wanted it on me just as it was, with its loose lines, and unpolished finish. I sent the picture to Jaye and asked if I could get it done on May 8. Exactly two years to date that Josiah had tattooed "I love you more" on himself for me.

"Yes of course!" she would make it happen. I told no one, not a soul. This was some sort of ritual I was processing, not intentionally, it was just unfolding this way. I finally told my friend and massage therapist Heather, a week before during a massage. She had wanted to get something done herself, so she came with me. Probably a good thing I was not alone. Two hours before I left for Jaye's, I did tell Richard what I was doing, right after I had walked into my guest bathroom and found eleven cents on the counter. A dime and a penny. I picked it up, asked Rich if it was his. No one had been over and no; it was not his. I didn't think so, I knew it was from Josiah. Then as I was getting in the car to drive the one hour to Joshua Tree, the date he had drawn this for me popped off the picture. 10.3.11. No wonder I found eleven cents! I knew he was happy with what I was doing.

I laid on Jaye's table, embracing the love that was being etched onto my back, holding two essential oil blends in my hand, mostly because I was concerned I may get heartburn while laying on my stomach for so long. Then I realized these two oils were symbolic. Emotionally, each blend represented something. Digest-Zen was helping me with the capacity to digest this new reality I am living, and Citrus Bliss was allowing me to create my next present moment.

Jaye's artistic ability is impeccable. Her expression

of Josiah's drawing was perfection. I never realized the impact a tattoo could have when done with such intention.

One week later, I was walking toward my bedroom, when out of nowhere this thought dropped into my consciousness: "May 8th.... five, eight. This will be our Mother's Day. Yours and mine, Josiah!" And then, my knees hit the floor. My son left planet earth when I was fifty-eight years old!

22 and the Mini Horses

March of 2017, Richard, and I moved into a new home. We had wanted to move from Southern California after he retired. I gave it my best, "Sure, that sounds wonderful," try for two years. We traveled to northern California and Oregon numerous times, looking for that perfect retirement spot, where our kids would come, and the grandkids could play. However, Thanksgiving of 2016 gave us one more grandchild, a little tiny girl. I was supposed to be at that birth, she was supposed to wait a week for me. Rich had promised, (like he would really know,) that the baby would not come while I was away. Well, she did.

That same day we saw what most people would call the home of their dreams. Yet as the phone rang, somewhere around three a.m., and my heart leaped and sank simultaneously, I knew there was no way I could move out of state. So, we moved locally instead, to a smaller version of our dream, and stayed close to our true dream. Our children. I could not wait for Josiah to come see my new pad. His advice to me in his adult life, especially the last few years, and about moving, were, "Do whatever you want, Mom, whatever makes you happy!" He understood the stress and fears I had been carrying, and there was nothing he could do to change his mother's heart. So, he would encourage me to enjoy my life. I did not have an iPhone, so no video chatting for me. I figured out how to go live on Facebook with only one person! I was so excited, and we set up a time I could travel through my new space with him. The phone was vibrating in my hand. I could feel his excitement to come, experience what I was experiencing and call this home his own. Less than three months later, he would come for a visit. His last summer with me and the most brutal and painful yet, fulfilling summer of my life. My new home has a stable. A stable? How is Spirit providing this for us? We had talked about getting miniature animals, a donkey or horse, after we settled into Richard's retirement, and now, we had the place for them. Just not quite yet!

Josiah's summer came and went and before I knew it, I was in this new vibration, the energy of grief. The outdoors seemed foreign; I was navigating the unimaginable. Three months had passed; the new year had come, and "I love you more" tattoos were done.

The Minis

I was still solemn. Rich reminded me of the mini horse rescue that was forty-five minutes from our home. "Let's go check it out!" he encouraged. We set up a time, grabbed my oldest granddaughter and headed to the ranch of mini elves and fairies, at least that is how they appear to me. There were hundreds of them. Adorable tiny horses, some loving and some sad and withdrawn from their previous lives that had devastated them and brought them here. I was enchanted.

On our way home, Monica, my life-long horsy friend's daughter, called me. "Do you want to come over to my mom's and see some sunshine? Mom just bought two mini horses!"

"What?" I exclaimed, "We are just coming home from getting some sunshine!" I went on to tell her where we had been, then, of course, we drove right over. Cindy had seen a sign from a ranch, just up the road, that were selling some of their mini horses, because of a relocation issue. Rich looked at me and said," Oh, no, you are not going up there to buy minis. We know nothing about them yet, let's keep going to the rescue!"

I said "Okay!" as Cindy dialed the number to the woman that owned the minis and told her I would be calling. Which I did as soon as I got home and set up a time to see her minis the following day, all while Richard said "No!" and he knew he was being overruled.

We headed out the next morning, a short twelve-minute ride up the hill to mini horse heaven. Marin met us at the gate and walked us back to the tribe of beauties. She had been a breeder and had shown many of the horses. Some were champions, and some were daughters of the champions. There must have been sixty or more gathering and greeting us. She showed us the daughter horses that were for sale. Immediately I was drawn to a strawberry roan named Chloe. As I spoke to her, I began to sing to her, "Gypsy Woman!" I knew she was mine. I fell in love with a couple other mares, but I was hellbent on getting a boy, a gelding. You know, a mother and son team. But all her boys were young, ungelded, and untamed. For the next five months I went up every week, sometimes twice a week, to visit my Gypsy and the other minis, always in hope that one day, one of those boys would fall in love with me. No luck. I knew I had to get Gypsy a companion from Marin. These horses had been together for years and if I was going to separate them, then they needed to know who they were going with.

22

The number 22 was beginning to let itself be known. Josiah was constantly bringing my awareness to 22. He left on the 22nd, I got that, but was there more to this? I was aware that Angels connect with us through numbers, and each number has a meaning. I looked up the number 22 and its meaning. Angel number 22 encourages you to work diligently on your spiritual path and soul purpose. To be balanced and live in harmony. To be strong in your convictions. Just as the gray in the feathers had shown me, and how Josiah chose to live his life. In numerology, 22 is considered one of the most powerful numbers. It represents balance and is a creative master builder. Josiah is a master builder. He had said those exact words to Jeremy in his letter. There was the message of the orange in the feather. There is more meaning to the number 22, but I did not need any more of it. Josiah was not only telling me what 22 represented to the angels and numerology, and what he wanted for me, but why he chose it and how he was going to remind me every single day that the number 22 was, without question, a sign from him.

My son's Cyr wheel had been tucked away in the garage. One day I felt like I had been slapped on the head and stopped in front of the blue bag that encased the five parts of his wheel.

"Raina!" I lectured myself, "Why isn't this in your healing room?"

I immediately picked up the bag and proceeded to take it in my room. I unzipped the bag and took out each golden part of his magic. It took me forever to uncase them, as each one held such treasured memories. I began to click each part into the next when I noticed they all had numbers on them. They were marked with numbers telling its size, that it was food grade material, where it was made, Canada, what looks like a serial code, and the time it was made; 22:20. I gasped and told Josiah, out loud. "Oh my gosh, Josiah! This is way too much for me to handle by myself!" I felt immobile, as I looked at all five parts. Each one displaying the same, 22:20. I sat down on the floor, well, I probably fell to be more accurate, sobbing uncontrollably.

A few days after that, Kelly, Josiah's dear friend, was coming for a visit. A first-time face-to-face meeting. Kelly was the one who contacted me and told me about her dream, as I was driving to Santa Cruz to get him. She and Josiah had a close bond, and he was now gifting her to me. He had made sure she knew how special she was to him by leaving her dimes also. One morning she noticed a dime ring on the table. A ring that was made from a dime! She talked with everyone she could think of that had been at her home, and not one person could claim it. She knew it had to be from Josiah!

When Kelly arrived, I took her into my healing room to show her the Cyr wheel and tell her the story. As my words were leaving my mouth about the 22s, Kelly's eyes widened as she pointed to the clock, "Look! It is 2:22! In unison, we both began to cry. My son was crying too. His ethereal tears of joy that Kelly and I had made our way to each other.

The Blending

I had to show Kelly the minis. I told her of my dilemma. How I wanted a boy, but that just wasn't' manifesting. She told me, "You just need to get her best friend!" I knew she was right; Marin and Rich had been saying the same thing. But I wanted a boy, damn it! I had narrowed the mares down to two of them, Wisteria, a chocolate mini and Mary, a tiny pinto. I took Kelly to see Gypsy first. Gypsy knew me well already and perked up when she heard me singing. I had no doubt about her. I could feel Josiah's presence in her when I would tell her my woes. Then I took her to meet Wisteria. She was lovely and the grandkids loved this one too, but something inside of me abruptly said, "No!" I then took her over to see tiny Mary. I was standing in front of her while Kelly was brushing her mane. I bent down to get close to her face and told her, "You are so cute, you are just so cute!"

Mary began to nuzzle me and put her nose on my

shoulder! "Look Kelly! Look how cute she is!"

Kelly's heart spoke, "We just need a sign!" and I kid you not, at the second her words left her lips, a ladybug came out of Mary's mane and landed on Kelly's dime ring! "Raina, did you see that!"

Of course, I *had* seen it! I stood up. My body was filled with my son. I could hear him saying, *"Her, Mom! I want her!"* I walked a little to see if Mary would follow me. She did. I walked a little again, you know, just to test it. She came to me again. "Of course, you want her Josiah! She is tiny, an elf. Exactly what I should have known you would have wanted all along."

I sent Rich a picture of Mary with the words, "I'm really feeling this one!"

"Is that Mary?" he texted.

"Yes, she is so sweet, kissing my face and following me, totally adorable!"

"You liked her from the start," he replied.

"Yes, I have, she was exceptional today!"

"Then do it," he said. "Remember, Marin told us Mary and Chloe (Gypsy) were best friends!"

He was right. She had told us that. I finally had peace about which horses were my healing companions. Not a mom and son, not what I thought I wanted, but better. What Josiah and the Spirit realm had chosen for me. Best friends. Mary needed her spirit name also. But what was going to represent Josiah? Mariah? Fairy? I tussled with something that had the flare of my Spirit child, and had a "Y" or "EE" on the end so it still rolled out to Marys' ears, her identity. Then it hit me. Josiah, my Elf Alchemist. What was the feminine form of Elf, which she clearly was? "Elvy." The meaning of the name Elvy is Elf Warrior. Perfect. My Fairy, "Gypsy Love," and My Elf, "Elvy Alchemy," had been decided.

Confirming 22

A couple months passed, and my friend Nancy Myers and I had a lunch date. Nancy is another mother with a son in Spirit. I met Nancy early on in this journey at a meditation at the home of another friend, Virginia. Nancy began taking pictures after her son Robbie left this planet, and orbs began to appear in every picture. Her story is fascinating, I will include a link to her in the resource part of this book. This is something special, that none of us knew we wanted, until we were given it, the friendships of Spirit moms. During our lunch, I told Nancy about the mini horse story and the number 22. Then she blew my mind.

"You know, everything that has to do with Mary Magdalene is in 22s."

"Really?" I questioned. I'd had no idea.

The day the Catholic church celebrates their feast day for her is July 22nd. Written the way the Europeans write it is 22/7. There is so much sacred geometry around Mary Magdalene and the number 22. It was undeniably interesting, but with so much mathematics it was hard to comprehend. Yet there was a connection Josiah wanted me to understand. 22 and the minis name was Mary. A week or so later, while chatting with Virginia, I went on to tell her about the mini story and the number 22, along with Nancy's story about Mary Magdalene.

"You know," Virginia added, "Everything that has to do with the Merkabah vibrates to the number 22." (Merkabah is the divine light vehicle to connect with the higher realms. "Mer" means Light. "Ka" means Spirit. "Ba" means Body. Mer-Ka-Ba is a three-dimensional star of David!) Are you kidding me right now! Josiah had created a Merkabah, out of wood, up in Portland, at his OneDoorLand home and they did a video skit in the Jewish cemetery, looking for the Merkabah. He had it tattooed on him, along with the Kabbalah's tree of life! What was happening right now? My mind was looping in circles with all this input! We hung up and I began to search for name numbers. The Merkabah is a three-dimensional star of David. What is David's number? It lit up the page! 22! I kept searching. The Hebrew alphabet is made up of 22 letters, which are used to compose the Word of God. (remember our Hebrew tattoo?) The word of God is called a lamp. (Proverbs 6:22), thus it is the light by which we are to live. Josiah and I always referred to God, Source, The creator, or the Universe, as The Light! The word light is found 264 times in Scripture. When 264 is divided by 12 (divine authority,) we have 22, which represents light! What? Are you serious right now? Oh, and God created 22 things in the six days of creation. At least that is the biblical version! So here I am, mind blown and asking myself, What is Josiah's middle name? David! When did he leave? On the 22nd! What was the name of the horse he wanted? Mary! His wheel with 22:20 or, basically, 222. Remember, it was 2:22 on the clock as I told the 22 story. He was showing me loud and clear, *"Mom, I am here, I am here, see me in this alchemy as well as the others. I am the number, '22.'"* As much as my mind was blown, it was also noticeably clear. Every day without fail, I would get his sign, 22, a reminder that, "He loves me," and I could tell him, "I love you more!" and the next time I would see, "22," He would simply be saying, "More!" and I would say, "More than More!" because Mom always wins. Our earthly dialogue would continue every time I saw 22! The Light of Love.

Summer Returned and Josiah's birthday
Legoland

The minis would distract me from the summer remembered. But distractions are temporary, as I am sure you know. There were twinkles, or sparks of calm, I had forgotten were part of my persona, but the last summer had been brutal, and every cell in my body remembered it. June would turn into July, and my cells would remember, I had just driven home with him. Why didn't I force him to stay with me a little longer? "Stop it Raina," I would chastise myself. "He is magic, let him be magic!" July would bring in August. His birthday month. His 30th birthday. Birth, the one thing I had done right. Each one was perfect, and I recovered without one bit of issue. I am not supposed to have given birth to you, and then not be able to share your birthday with you! But before Josiah's birthday, we had a six-year-old to celebrate.

Legoland was the destination of my youngest grandson's birthday. Legoland is extremely busy, I would be pressed to get a sign there. Yet without fail, Josiah would make his presence known. There is a boat ride at Legoland where you can steer your own boat through, what they call the "open waters." I was riding with my ten-year-old grandson Blaze. He was hoping for the red boat. His favorite color. Our boat was pulling in, and it was indeed the red one. Blaze was ecstatic. We hopped in and he took hold of the steering wheel. Our eyes turned forward now, we could see the front of our personal ship and its number: 22! Once more this kid of mine was pulling strings that surpassed my ability for reason. Later that year when I was shopping for Christmas, I would find a red-hot wheels car for Blaze with, you guessed it, 22 as its number!

Ever Josiah Tree

Now back to the reality of my plight. Josiah's birthday. Jeremy's in-laws had given me a small orange tree in November to honor Josiah, and a memorial plaque with his name. The plaque stayed inside, and the tree sat at the back door. I was unable to plant it where it would get the most sunlight. It was too far from my sight. I needed the tree close. Finally, on my birthday in March, Rich asked me if I was ready to plant it. That poor tree had sat for almost five months in its pot that was stunting its growth. I was not up for much else, but how was I going to see it in the dark?

We drove to Walmart to buy solar lights that I could circle the tree with, to illuminate it at night. Did I have it in my head that if the tree were too far, and I could not see it, I would not be able to see Josiah either? If you do not do one thing, it will not trigger the next? With the movement of the orange tree, it did trigger something! Something positive!

"Rich?" I called to him, "Why can't that tree be Josiah's tree?"

The tall aged evergreen that lived right outside my healing room window was calling me now, and I could hear it.

"Of course, it can be, I will redo the bricks for you and Josiah!" As he prepared the ground around the evergreen, ever Josiah tree, I went to the store to find ornaments that would decorate it. Of course, the heavens opened, and I found exactly what I wanted. Three windchimes, the tree of life, a lotus flower, and the hamsa hand. I found stars, butterflies, and an angel dish for all the dimes. I came back home to see the tree had been loved by Rich and made ready for me. I hung the chimes, gathered rocks and crystals from the house and laid them on the ground around it. I set the memorial plaque intended for the orange tree there against the tree in full view.

I called the kids and told them, "I want to have a gathering, Josiah would want a gathering." Then the most bizarre sentence came out of my mouth! "Can it just be adults? I need to be able to be off duty that day!"

"Of course," they all agreed, but I knew I had blown all my kids away. Come on? No grandkids? I knew I did not have enough in me to be the hostess with the mostess, as they say, but I could do a gathering. I invited my cast of characters that had been steadfast and unwavering, the ones who had stayed close this last year and had my kids do the same. It was a beautiful blend of family and friends. Josiah's best friend from Prescott drove here to see me, and his best friend from high school stayed 'til the last. And Rain drove eight hours to be with me, ready to do my bidding. And I did have a bidding.

There were hundreds of heartfelt messages that had streamed in from around the world. The people in the stories he had shared with me now became even more vivid, with their voices echoing his. Deep thoughts and memories filled his page, and my inbox. Being inside their memories became the warm cushion I would rest on. Throughout the year it would continue. Surprise visits from Josiah were shared within the computer and I wanted them in a book.

Rain was determined to make it happen for me. She combed through his pages. Copying, and pasting all the love into a document, we could send to Staples to create this book. I wondered if I had given her the task that would destroy her heart, or fulfill it? Mindfully I would check in on her to see she was holding back her tears, and I knew it was for me. I was asking a lot from her. She had already done so much. One month prior, one of Josiah's friends Bryn, tagged me on a picture on Facebook. It was a painting of a spirit man meditating in the desert.

The resemblance to Josiah was uncanny. The man who posted it was Heyoka! Heyoka? Akoya backwards? What are the chances? I quickly posted it. Pointing out the name of who posted it, and asking everyone, "Can you see him?" Yes! Of course, they could! Then down in the comments, John the Flute maker's wife Cathy gave me the artist's name. Cathy is quite the artist herself, but how in the world did she find who painted this? Technology?!

I sent the picture to Rain and told her the story. I looked up the artist and sent him an email, sharing with him how much this painting meant to me and the uncanny resemblance to my son, with pictures of Josiah to prove my point. He graciously wrote me back. He could see it too but was in the middle of relocating because of the northern fires. I told him I would contact him again after he settled to get a print.

Meanwhile, Rain was doing the same, except she took it one step further. She did order a print. Framed it and gave it to me for his birthday. Now I was asking more of her and she was doing it, without a tear for me to see. She emailed the book to Staples the day before the gathering. I wanted it there, visible for us all to read. At Staples, the clerk and Rain were dialoging when I noticed a huge numbered sign behind the desk. It was the number of their next project to be completed. A huge 22 in bold black print stared back at us, becoming the backdrop of our heartfelt photoshoot. Rain knew there would be more to add to the book, so she purchased an extra box of the colored paper we had used. One hundred sheets. In the book, there were eleven unused sheets still. One hundred eleven sheets left, or 222, both sides.

The gathering was a balance of tears and laughter. I was grateful to hear the stories of my son. I had asked my guests to bring a chime, an ornament, or a rock to put at the Ever Josiah tree. Aimee has given me several gifts to warm the heart of this grieving mother. A blanket with a collage of Josiah's pictures on it for my birthday, and a puzzle, with every family member she could put in it for Mother's Day. She said it was to put back the pieces of my life.

I saved it for Josiah's birthday, and had it out, for all who loved him to put the pieces back with me. The puzzle was half done. Pieces were still scattered when my daughter Valerie sat down at the kitchen table, determined to mend the puzzling pieces of my heart. I knew she would. Her heart was as broken as mine.

The day was finally over. I thought maybe I had made it. But I woke the next morning, no baby. I had made a great distraction on his birthday, the day I would have given birth, but the morning was quiet, I was empty-handed.

"Can I get a sign, babe?" Had he not given me enough? I cried like a baby when Rain was standing by her car to leave; then we heard a flutter. I looked up into those same trees that Josiah had visited us in butterfly form, just days after his ascension. And there he was! That same butterfly! This time there were no marks, and both his little legs were intact.

"Rain!" I turned her to look, "Josiah!"

This magnificent butterfly stayed still as we told him how much we loved him, missed him and how grateful we were for this moment! We looked on, frozen in awe, until Josiah allowed the butterfly to flutter on its way. I held her, as if I were holding him. Not wanting to let go, and knowing she had her own voyage to travel.

August 31, 2018

Where have I been? Drowning in the ocean that consumes my inner thoughts. I am a giant ocean liner in the middle of the ocean with no dry land in sight. I am all by myself and I do not have the faintest idea how to navigate this beast. And to where? Where am I supposed to go? And what will I do when, and if I get there?

I live within a new normal I did not desire. My heart dense with emotions and tears. My every waking moment ponders the presence of you. I gaze in all directions. I listen with perched ears. My body alert to all its senses. My light, my love, my deep connection to you, now filtered by the denseness of life. I seek to remove layers between us, soul to soul, heart to heart, I find you.

September Concert, O.A R and the Airport

Those years in college were amazing for Josiah. He acted, designed theater sets, and as always, turned me onto his favorite bands. We were in the season of O.A.R., which stands for "Of A Revolution." He found out they were playing at the House of Blues Anaheim, and insisted we go. The House of Blues is probably one of the coolest venues in Orange County. We muscled our way towards the front and sang our hearts out. I loved how he loved to share his world with me, how all my children feel at ease with me.

A year later they were playing again, this time at The House of Blues Hollywood, even cooler than Anaheim. This time his college friend Deonna would join us. We arrived at the venue way too early to go inside. The bouncer suggested we go around to the other parking lot entrance. There, another bouncer invited us into the lounge area, and basically backstage. Josiah was beside himself as we walked past the open door that the band members were getting ready for the show in. We entered the most bohemian hip lounge. Josiah, only nineteen at the time, thought he would test the waiter, and it worked. The waiter did not card him, and he was even more thrilled.

I know, you are thinking, *she let him drink?* Do not worry, neither Josiah nor I are drinkers, however much I wish I could drown out this year. We shared the one sneaky drink, and off we went, back through the open doors of the band members, down the stairs and into the concert. My son was walking on air. O.A.R.'s song "Heard the World" would become our hearts' cry after his diagnosis. The chorus alone brings us to our knees!

I heard the world up late night

Holding my breath tight

Trying to keep my head on right

There's a chill in the air

Nobody could care how we're

Caught up in the fight of your life

We were caught up in the fight of our lives! Trying to keep our head on right! And now it is just me! Right around my birthday, I read that O.A.R. was going to be at the House of Blues Anaheim. What? During this first year, O.A.R. appears? I thought maybe Deonna would want to go with me. I had not seen her in years. Did she still live near Orange County? I left it on the back burner while I planted the orange tree and got through the day.

Two weeks later, Deonna messaged me. "Hi Raina! I must have delayed memory going on, but I wanted to wish you a Happy Birthday back when it actually was your birthday and it just triggered in my head now! I hope you felt the love pour in, and took some time to celebrate yourself."

We dialogued back and forth about Josiah, and then I told her, "O.A.R. is coming to the House of Blues in September." She immediately went to their site to purchase the tickets for us. I talked to my sister about a hotel nearby and we were set to relive a memory and honor Josiah. As the concert drew near, I began to feel anxious, almost panicked as I listened to them on my iPod, onto which Josiah had downloaded all their music for me so many years ago. I searched for "Heard the World," and blurrily drove down the 57 freeway. I realized if they played that song, I would lose it. I might need to be hauled out of there. I shut it off before it ended and cleared my vision. Crashing would only make things worse. I was thrilled to see Deonna. A vision of days past, and a goddess walking towards me. We reminisced as we strolled to the concert. Her young mind straightening out my mixed-up memories of the concerts. I warned her about "Heard the World," and she totally understood.

Two other bands played before O.A.R., both of which amazed us. I felt joy and apprehension as O.A.R. walked on stage. Tears welled as I asked Josiah to join us. To my amazement, they did not play "Heard the World." They did even better. The lead singer started to explain their new song, about the people who leave this planet too soon, called "Miss you all the time!" which would be released the following month.

I looked over at Deonna in shock. "Deonna, did you hear all that? It will be released basically on the one-year anniversary of Josiah's ascension?"

Then the band began to play.

You know that I don't like to say goodbye

I didn't know that we were out of time

I'm sorry that I couldn't save your life

So I walk, yeah I walk

I go to pick the phone up every day

And imagine conversations we would say

But I'm always hanging up the same way

And I walk, yeah I walk

In the house where the heart don't cry

Dancing in a silver light

And I'm dreaming of you tonight

I miss you all the time

All the stars are calling out your name

Ever since you went away

There's no sleeping you off my mind

I miss you all the time

I miss you all the time

I know that you were only passing through

In a moment you were lighting up the room

There will never be another like you

So I walk, yeah I walk

And I try to keep my eyes up on the road

And remember all the stories that you told

But I'm sorry that you'll never grow old

So I walk, yeah I walk

In the house where the heart don't cry

You're dancing in a silver light

And I'm dreaming of you tonight

I miss you all the time

All the stars are calling out your name

Ever since you went away

There's no sleeping you off my mind

I miss you all the time

I miss you all the time

I miss you

I miss you

I miss you all the time

In the house where the heart don't cry

Dancing in the silver light

And I'm dreaming of you tonight

I miss you all the time

All the stars are calling out your name

Ever since you went away

There's no sleeping you off my mind

I miss you all the time

I miss you all the time

Yeah, I miss you all the time

Paralyzed except for our tears, we wept.

The following week I was traveling to Utah for an annual convention I knew was going to take its toll on me. I didn't want to go, but my friends lovingly insisted and said, "Let's fly, it will be easier." Driving did seem too hard this year. It was usually a wild adventure, but these days driving to Orange County almost took me out, never mind Utah. I am not a big fan of flying, though. I am a chicken and my nerves were evident.

We had been at the airport for a couple hours before they called us to board. The whole time we could hear that a radio was playing, but the words were un-recognizable with all the airport chatter. When they called us to board, I was the first to stand. A bit shaken, Kim looked at me, about to say, "You're okay!" when she saw my eyes get huge and my finger pointing upward.

"Do you hear that?" I asked.

"Hear what?"

"The song. It's O.A.R., the band I just saw with

Deonna. The one Josiah and I saw together. It is their song, "This Town!" I tuned everyone out for a brief moment and heard these words.

In the morning wake me up

And tell me everything

So I can understand your world

And you can understand my dream

Yeah, I could be anywhere

And you could be there with me

But I just want to be a ghost

And see everything

I don't want it to be the way they want it

This town, this night, this crowd

Come on put them up, let me hear it loud

This town, this city, this crowd

Stand up on your feet put your worry down

And every one of you all around

Come on y'all let's take this town

Let's take this town

It's better that we keep this close

Keep you close to me

Walking under every sky

Over every sea

And just like that, my fear faded away. He was with me. I knew I would be safe, under every sky and over every sea.

October 20, 2018
Two Nights Before the One-year Anniversary

DWELL

The sun dwindles down on my weary mind

When tomorrow arrives, will it have answers?

The day now here, my heart still heavy

I am missing who I am

And who I am dwells so far away

Raindrops from my silent heart fall softly

No one sees and I don't tell

Alone I sit missing where I am

And where I am dwells so far away

Pounding with anticipation

The day moves on

I hear a voice

A reflection of my own

Mirroring me, is you

Where you are, I want to be

But where you are dwells so far away

The day closing around me

The stars greet me

As the moon shines down

Reminding me that I am one day closer to where I am going

And where I am going is to dwell with you

~Raina

One Year: The Tattoo

A few days before that miraculous plane ride, I had been invited to write in the compilation book *52 Weeks of Gratitude*. When I got home from that convention, I sat down and my heart poured onto the yellow page legal pad I had placed in front of me. Word after word, I wrote without pausing. Three quarters of the way through, I began to doubt myself. I thought I should be writing about something else. How was I going to turn this into a story that would mend someone's heart, when writing it was breaking mine?

I have a boot box full of years of writing. Poetry and thoughts. All those words my mom found so charming. *Maybe I will find something to spark a new story,* I thought. I dug the box out from under other books and writings and brought it up to my table. Rummaging through the years of words always makes me laugh, and cry. What was I thinking when I wrote some of this minutia? I kept digging, reading, and finding nothing that made any more sense than what was already on paper. Then I lifted the last page to expose the bottom of the box, and there lay a dime! A dime! I had not been in this box for years. It was in the closet, covered. A dime!

"Josiah!" Tears pooled my eyes. "Josiah, I will continue." I took the dime and placed it next to my pad of paper and continued. He was polishing my pain. Edited and submitted, Jeremy and Valerie showed up on Oct 17, five days before the one-year, to get our one-year ceremonial tattoo – his artist's signature, Josiah Akoya. We had it planned for a long time. I wanted it on the

22nd, but Jaye was unavailable that day and you already know, it had to be Jaye. So, I navigated for Oct 17th, the last day Josiah and I had messaged on the phone. The last message I got from him was a heart emoji, and a heart was going on me that day too. We had gotten what we had put on us, the "I love you more" in Hebrew tattoo, from a wooden plaque he had made for me. The other side had the signature we would use for the ceremony. I found a carved heart on another piece of his art. I asked Jaye to tattoo him back into my "Ovary."

You know, because that is where he needs to be, right?

As I was getting ready, I placed Josiah's necklace over my head; it's a Triple spiral or triskele. He had bonded two iolites to one side of it that I place towards my heart. He loved iolite, it had become one of his favorite stones because it is useful in enhancing your intuition and deepening your meditation. It can also help you gain insight and connect you to your higher self and enhance your creative vision. I understood his love for it. I was pretty sure it was helping me too.

On this day I became aware that I had been almost unconsciously wearing it every day. In that awareness I told him, "I guess I have been wearing this every day, son!" I caressed the spiral triskele in my hand. "Josiah, I don't think I can stop wearing this at one year!"

One of the iolites fell into my hand. I looked at my hand in disbelief and slowly opened it, then a rush of the most beautiful energy breathed through me. Being the possessive mother I am, I replied, "I am going to wear it until you have the second iolite fall out!"

I heard voices; my kids had arrived. Before we left, I read them my story, which they had no idea I was writing. The timing was perfect, Josiah was present. This tattoo I knew would be black, I had given Jaye some of Josiah's ashes to mix with the ink, hence the ceremony and me wanting him tattooed back into my womb. I now have three matching tattoos with my daughter, two with Jeremy and "I love you more" with Josiah. Will I tattoo more of his tattoos on me, time will only tell.

The day Kim Richardson, my publisher for *52 weeks of Gratitude,* announced the date of the book release, was the same day O.A.R. announced "Miss You all the Time" would be released. Another synchronistic moment and more tears than I thought were possible. My story in *52 Weeks,* "Polished Through the Pain," is the Introduction of this book.

The following year, Kim announced she was gathering authors for her second compilation book titled, "Kindness Matters." When I thought about kindness, the first thought I had, was how unkind I had been to myself. I had beaten myself up about not doing this, or that, for Josiah and it had plagued me deeply. I had been so hard on myself; Josiah came to tell me not to be. I sat down to write and within four hours my story was on paper and ready to send to Kim. I knew there had been someone other than myself writing this story titled, "Gentle Rain."

" Love, light and peace surrounds us with color."

~ Josiah " Akoya" David

Gentle Rain

Unfathomable with the hidden parts of my soul I cry, the gentle rain from my broken heart beckons for absolution. From exhaustion I beg for slumber that shuns me.

This mantra replaced the hymn I once sang. My beautiful twenty-nine-year-old son had been stolen from me, the earth and its forest had swallowed him. It was a warm October Sunday in 2017. Josiah, my youngest child thought today was as perfect as any other day, so perfect that he thought a motorcycle ride deep into the forest of Santa Cruz would only enhance the journey of his day. He straddled the bike, owning the road he would travel. Deep within the forest, I believe the tree elves beckoned him, as they caught his attention, he realized they were showing him a portal, a doorway to the spirit realm. Josiah loved the Earth Elements, the Sky Angels and anything that spoke of higher dimensions, so it is without question he wanted to go the way they beckoned, leaving his body and the motorcycle unattended, it met the tree that sealed the portal.

Is this the fairytale I tell myself or is this the truth of the Elements, the Angels, Spirit, and the Universe that compels us? His entrance to Spirit, my entrance to unimaginable sorrow. A pain with an identity that demanded attention. Left to its own will, it would have consumed me and led me directly to that same portal.

Who am I now? I am no longer me, I am grief, doubling as wife, mother, grandmother, sister, and friend. When you experience someone so close to you, someone who is truly a part of your very existence leaves this planet, it stops you, stunts you, the un-answered questions haunt you, you turn inward towards guilt and despair and I should have and why didn't I, play on a loop. Everything about you is in question.

I had to find the answers.

What does this have to do with kindness? Every-thing.

We have all experienced the profound despair that leaves us broken and beating ourselves up. Taking responsibility for other people's stories, making it our fault and creating such unkindness within ourselves.

If only I would have called him that morning, he would have told me he was going on that ride and I could have harassed him into not going... If only I would have forced him to do this differently or that... If only I would have loved him more. Why didn't I call, oh G-d, why didn't I call him?

Tears pouring inward as well as outward, each one producing more guilt and responsibility than the next. "Josiah I am so sorry," I lamented. Walking across the family room of my home after speaking out loud how guilty I felt, I picked up my Talking to Heaven cards. As I shuffled them a card fell to the floor facing upwards so I could see it. I inhaled and held my breath as if I would never breathe again, yet he was pressing me to breathe and continue.

The card read: "It is not your fault."

I fell to my knees, uncontrollably weeping as I press-ed the card against my chest that once held my heart, "Josiah," I bellowed, "How is this possible?"

I laid on the floor until the pouring turned to the gentle rain of calm. When I finally stood up, I felt hungry, I glanced around the room, bewildered. Had I eaten today? And if I had, was it something other than peanut butter, pita chips or coffee? My grief was so prominent all else was excluded, including taking care of me. I had stopped being kind to myself, how can kindness matter if I didn't? If I'm not kind to myself, who's going to be?

Josiah is not here with me in the physical and that is unnervingly heart-wrenching. That will never go away, in truth I never want it to. I never want to not feel the magnitude of who he is, and what he represents to me, and my family and the impact he had and continues to have on all of us. Let the tears flow, the continuous gentle rain of love, not guilt and responsibility. Sorrow mixed with the jewel of Josiah, his siblings, my grandchildren and all the love that surrounds me, I walked into the kitchen. Staring into the refrigerator, I am still not hungry. Laughter was going to take some time to return. It was going to take over a year before I could truly exercise again and be physically present in my body. I wasn't going to feel right for a while, but I was going to stop telling myself I did something wrong.

We had a destiny; I signed a contract with him. This time he was my son, last time I'm pretty sure he was my father, but none of that matters, what matters is that he and I continue. Not as we were but as we are now. Without kindness to myself, and giving myself grace in the line of fire, I would not have been able to continue. I had to be thoughtful to myself and give myself some sympathy and understanding for the new me.

Dark despair, trauma, and even drama create the next version of our tapestry. Weaving through our hearts with golden threads, filling in the broken lines.

I understand I had to feel every one of those tortured emotions, they must be dealt with. Everything I, we, go through defines us. Life dictates and we must take notes. Pondering the pain is necessary. The beatings we give ourselves are far worse than what others could give us. Life can be so cruel; we must not be cruel to ourselves.

My relationship with my son in Spirit is strong, mixed with tears, agony, amazement and gratitude. I would not be able to see this if I stayed in shame and blame. Does it rear its disgustingly ugly head at me? Yes! I am not going to lie to you. I'm human, a mother, devastated by the unimaginable. Yet out of what we cannot imagine, we press on to imagine something boundless. The ability to survive through sorrow and find our way back to the ones we thought were out of reach.

Love has no limit and death is an illusion. A symphony of painful chords. And if we can see this pain as our own portal, a doorway to our higher dimension. That those same Tree Elves and Sky Angels that beckoned my son, are also beckoning me to a place where unconditional love abounds? Wouldn't that, then, include unconditional love for myself? Why yes, it would.

I forced myself to eat. I had forgotten how good food tasted. I had forgotten the clarity that comes from nourishing myself. I looked outside the window; the sun was shining. Even the outdoors seemed foreign. I took my journal outside and invited vitamin D from the sun's rays onto my skin. The thunderstorm of my soul began to still. My pen began to dance across the blue that lined the pages, creating words that were not mine.

"Breathe, just breathe, Raina. There has been too much going on in your head. You have logged everything, and it is wearing you thin. Be, just be. There are still moments to be had that Josiah will be with you in, I promise, it is not over. He is here and will be with you in all things you do, outside with your animals, and inside your spirit. Breathe. Take in the newness of his energy. He is asking you to pause and feel him, pause and see him, pause and hear him. Dry your tears, Raina, he is here. Close your eyes, Raina, he is here. See him. Open your heart, Raina. Open it. Write. Let it in. Let in the new energy. Let this vibration in. It is Josiah!"

I looked down at the page before me. Who had written this? It was not from Josiah or it would have said Mom! Was it me, channeling me? Was it the Earth Elements or the Sky Angels? It didn't really matter. The message was clear. My son is here! He is with me and that was not going to change. What had to change was me. I had to give up the story I deemed my fault and give it back to the Universe.

I created another letter. It had all my misconstrued interpretations of my part, however it poured out of me, I let the floodgates open. Once I felt a shift, I knew I was done. I lit the fire pit that would dissipate the evidence of these false feelings. It's amazing how the universe responds. As I sat outside witnessing these emotions burning to ashes and wondering if I might have left a few notes inside myself for further beatings. A gentle rain began to sprinkle amid the embers. The tears of my heart collapsed the entire sky above me, gently cleansing me, and reminding me once more, that I *had* been heard.

December's Retreat and Lullaby Letters, 2018

Right after Josiah's thirtieth birthday gathering, I decided to peer into the internet to see if I could find somewhere I was brave enough to venture out for solace. As much as I wanted to take the next flight to anywhere, I was still too tethered to the security; I supposed my home possessed. Then I saw, The Elemental Wisdom Retreat, in my local mountains. Just a quick thirty-minute drive from my house. Two of my friends were hosting it. I had sat in on a couple of their talks before. Both possess such incredible wisdom, I felt sure, I too would find the wisdom I was seeking. Wisdom! One of my favorite words, and exactly what I call the gatherings and meditations I hold at my home. This had to be a sign.

I had braved the first year. Wrote "Polished through the Pain." Dressed up again for Halloween, to trick-or-treat with my grandchildren. Managed a second Thanksgiving and was trying so hard to make Christmas fun again for my grandchildren. They are the liquid gold that swims through my broken heart. But I needed something for me, and this was it.

I carpooled up with a lovely woman who looked like my mother, of course! Blankets of snow covered the ground. We were entering the purest expression that mother earth shares with us. The fire inside the cabin mixed with the warmth of the fifteen women that circled the room, was already vibrating healing towards my soul. I only knew the host, Kathy, and Christie. It felt good to be unknown. Watchful to the expressions we were all about to unfold to each other. The weekend would revolve around the teachings of the Dagara Tribe of Burkina Faso, West Africa. We were going to explore the tribe's system of the elements to understand the power of Fire, Water, Earth, Nature and Minerals. To gain a better understanding of who we are, and how we relate to our world.

The weekend was filled with stories, journaling, discussions, rituals and sisterhood. Each of us sharing the rarest parts of ourselves, exposing the unseen to the seen.

I had a deep visitation with Josiah during one of the meditations.

I saw Josiah. It was as if he entered from a space behind me, and was greeted by many. They looked like performers, who took both his arms and guided him towards a staircase full of other performers. I could only see the back of him, his hair was to his shoulders. I recognized his tattoos. I could feel his presence so strong! I could sense, He had somewhere they wanted him to be. He had something he was to get ready for, like he was being guided up to the stage.

It felt surreal. I did not feel like he was leaving me, just that he was showing me he had somewhere to go.

The second day, while journaling, I wrote this:

You are being transformed and remolded. There has

216

been much done and much progress. The turning and spinning is tiresome. Sometimes the clay must be re-formed when it is almost finished. But that does not deny the progress that was already present. The sculptor learned in the process, as the clay merge to be. You are the sculptor and the clay and the water and the air. You are all that is.

What was I writing here? That all progress is progress. Even if I have a setback. Even if I decide to start over. That does not negate the progress. That I am all the elements. Meaning, I have the ability to create my next present moment, and the next, and the next! That the power was within me!

It was a truly transformative weekend. We cried, laughed, and were awestruck by the profound insights we were all seeing within ourselves and each other. In two days, fifteen strangers had become part of my road map, that was beginning to tell-tale itself to me. Within these women, were two other mothers with sons in Spirit. Pierce and Lisa. I was dumbfounded that out of fifteen, three of us had sons who were now friends in the Spirit world! It was hard for me to grasp. I had met so many mothers this year and prior to Josiah's ascension. One of my closest friends' sons left this planet just two years prior. One year prior to that, her lifelong friends' son had also left. These boys had been friends growing up. Their mothers were best friends. I was perplexed by the irony and felt some sort of urgency to do something! But what?

I had only been back from the retreat for a few days, yet insistent to stay in contact with all these women, especially the mothers. Richard and I were planning a huge surprise for the grandkids. The previous Christmas I could barely breathe, channeling Josiah through the jilted tears I cried. This year we were hoping to take the sting out of the holiday. Rich had created a racetrack in the open area of our backyard. We had found two go carts, a couple hoverboards, and some hot wheels, the red car with the 22 on it included. No one was allowed in the backyard. Not even the older kids knew what was going on, except Brian, my bonus son, because *what happens with Brian stays with Brian!* Our motto since he was a teenager.

Two days before Christmas. I had my jacket on, purse over my shoulder to run out for last minute insanity shopping. Something I loathe. Truth. The high vibes and hurry make me nuts! Ready to walk out the door, I get a rush. A feeling of urgency! I pause and ask, "Am I not supposed to go out?" I had been thinking about forming a Facebook group for the heart of the mother since the retreat. I thought, "Let me just get through Christmas!" Now the thought of the group was concaving in on me. "What now?" I question Spirit and myself, "I am literally running out the door?" But it began to consume me. The word lullaby dropped into my head, "Lullaby? That is for babies," I retorted. I walked into my healing room, coat on, purse still over my shoulder and wrote this...

Lullaby Letters,
Letters from our Children in Spirit

"My name is Raina, and I created this group so we could come together in deep support. Sharing stories and signs

from our children. Good days and not so good days... I just want you to be free to be... Whatever that looks like... Some say that this is a club, but this is not a club! A club is something you join on purpose... This is a soul connection... We resonate from a frequency altered by this unimaginable disbelief we live with...

Our voice is the lullaby, the song our children listened to while here on this physical plane...

As we continue to sing to them, talk to them, be with them, our children sing to us. They write us letters every day, in words, songs, pennies, dimes, nickels, feathers, and in that intuition deep within us that know, that we know, that we know, that they are speaking to us...

This is a place where you can share what's going on in your life, what you're seeing, what you're feeling... A place to come and experience encouragement... Listening to others enhances our own conviction and confidence in knowing that we are seeing the same...

Our children stand beside us now... just in a different form... We are all energy...They are energy...

This is The UNIMAGINABLE.

We are present to it now... My hope is as we journey together, we enhance each other's awareness that Our Bonds Continue...

Please invite the "Hearts of the Mothers" that cross your path to join. The more we join together, the more our vibrations rise, and when our vibrations rise...

We are closer to them

I am here for you

Raina**

I sat back as the magnitude of what I just wrote sunk in, and the waterworks of my soul took root. This was a truth; this was something I could do; these were words that were not mine. They were the voices of our children, and the Hearts of their Mothers.

I took a deep breath, put my purse down, took off my coat and wiped my Alice Cooper face. I understood I was not going anywhere until I had created this space, for you, and for me, for the Heart of their Mother.

I *was* able to leave the house, eventually. I endured the crowds. The grandkids, and adult children were elated by our surprise to them, beyond my expectations, and that made me happy. I had put my pinky toe in the ocean of healing. Forging another part of this un-imaginable voyage on a ship to where? I listened to my gut and made a group.

I had trickled the idea to my retreat sisters – "I might write my own book!"– after I shared "Polished through the Pain" with them. Declaring once more, "My mother always said I should write a book!" Never in my wildest dreams would I have thought it would be about this.

Then, one morning after the retreat I was sitting on the floor sipping my coffee when I heard the con-versation between The Ethereal and Josiah! I jumped up, wrote it down and knew Josiah was taking the helm.

Because of my story in *52 Weeks,* I am in many authors' groups. I am privy to posts I may have not seen while veering through Facebook. Another author made mention of Shanda, my current publisher, and that coat-wearing, purse-holding rush of urgency was con-caving again. Clear as the sound of a voice standing right next to me I heard, *"Contact Shanda!"*

Fear gripped me and I looked to my right as if to address the invisible voice that was standing there! "UM! No! As much as I say I want to write a book, I do not know how! So, no!"

Anyone who knows my Josiah knows he is persistent! Especially when he wants something, and without question, from me. The rush intensified and within seconds I was writing to her. We set up a time to talk. I figured that would seal the "I am not equipped to write a book theory" I had deemed my truth. On the contrary, she was intrigued by my stories about Josiah's Alchemy, and impressed by my words in *52 Weeks of Gratitude.*

I gave myself a month to consider what I was taking on. Josiah would not give me that month. Within days I called her back and agreed. I had to do this. "Oh dear goodness, why do I have to do this?" I wrestled. Then it hit me. Josiah had already asked me to, *"Tell My Story, I know you can't tell it all, but make them laugh, share my triumphs and my love!"* when I was writing his Tribute of Life.

"Let your voice show you your deepest shadows and why they exist. Allow understanding to transform these thoughts to help you strengthen the light that shines so brightly within. Train your mind to be disciplined in knowing the truth of you. Bless!"

~ Josiah "Akoya" David

January 2019

Sometimes I ask him why he left me, and then sometimes I can say I know why. He knew staying was never the option. Deep within him, he knew. He covered it up with his brilliance, and his ability to make you see how right the direction he was heading in was! He had the ability to realign my thinking with his, like a snake charmer that plays his magical flute, beckoning the cobra to obey. Josiah's voice and convincing wisdom charmed my heart and beckoned me to realign with his, so he could continue his journey with Mom's blessings, something he insisted upon. He had to have me aligned with his direction in order for him to continue. Sometimes our dialogue of wills would appear. The two cobras heads would come out of the woven basket to dance, the sacred shuffle of his charm and to redirect my wants and convince me he was the charmer, he was the weaver of his basket, and he is the one who plays the flute!

HELLO, February 12, 2019

I was back in my healing room, quietly contemplating before I started writing that morning, when all of a sudden I heard a muffled voice say, "Hello!"

I immediately grabbed my pen and wrote this:

Dear Mom,

I got the word out to your ear.

I know you heard it; I am getting stronger! You are getting stronger! We are getting stronger!

Our link is inseparable. Moving forward in the destination we have always been heading.

Do not look elsewhere, you are moving in the right direction. You are going at the right pace. You are diligent, and I am here saying, "Hello!"

Hello Son,

Yes, I heard you!

I still feel weary. My strength fades to dim more often than anyone knows.

I keep it silent. A quiet hush of despair creeps its way towards me, I embrace it before it consumes me. Thank you for seeing through that.

I sat back, astonished! Had I really just heard my son? Would this continue? Was I dreaming? No, I was awake and present, sitting upright in my chair! I had truly heard, "Hello!"

"*If you are running in search of something, you will never find it, because what you are looking for is not running. It is in plain sight. It sits and waits patiently. Running around means running within, which means, not being within. Bring stillness around you and enjoy stillness within. Love and light surround you. Peace, love and life embodies the universe.*"

~ Josiah "Akoya" David

Disneyland, 2019
Merging Energy

Here I go, venturing myself towards Disneyland. His land. The happiest place on earth, so they say. Will everything remind me of him? "Oh G-d, what was I thinking?"

I rumble through the specifics of this decision. I had not even questioned myself when Valerie announced she was taking the kids to Disneyland for their birthdays. "I want to go!" flew out of my mouth faster than the speed of light, immediately reliving one of the most jubilant memories of my life. Valerie and Josiah were in their early teens when the California Hopper became available. Two parks for the price of one. A special opportunity that Disney would give Californians, but only for a window of time. Perfect for a mini vacation. Vacations were rare for us back then, so I, without hesitation, wanted to have this experience with Valerie and my grandkids. I only had one pause. Maybe Valerie wanted her own adventure, without Mom! She has the same fondest to this memory, so I would totally get it if she wanted it for herself. I sheepishly asked her if she wanted what I had experienced, as she was getting in her car to leave for home, just in case she took me up on my question, I needed my disappointment to be unseen, but without a moment's hesitation, she wanted me with her. Inviting myself was welcomed.

I pulled up to the hotel and pulled the ticket to park. The first thing I noticed was 3/3. It was March 3rd, and as you know already, I see in numbers.

I broadcast, "It's 3/3, just saying, you guys!" By now they get me and expect random outbursts of numbers, words, or visuals I see as signs.

We head to the front desk. The clerk hands us our room number, 322! "Valerie!" I exclaimed. My daughter's eyes became so huge they swallowed her face. The rest of the evening was earthy; my sister came and picked us up and we headed for a noisy dinner at a busy restaurant. Back at the hotel we hung out, watched some TV. The usual things you do while hanging with kids in a hotel at night. Then I saw a message on my phone. It was from Tracy, the group facilitator of a group I had recently found online, Helping Parents Heal. She was welcoming me to the group.

My focus immediately shifted to converse with her. I wrote her back telling her a tiny bit of how I came to find her group, after I had created mine. I had not even thought of finding a group in the beginning of this journey, I only knew I had to find Josiah. As Tracy and I instant messaged back and forth, it became clear we had some unique similarities. Not just that we both had sons in Spirit, but they both had ascended at 29. We talked of our tattoos, signs, and people we knew in common. The conversation was outstanding in my mind. Now this might not sound like a sign to you, but it is. These kinds of kismet connections, raise our vibration in such a way that you sense the hand of your child in it. I finally fell asleep and had the most powerful experience I had ever had.

I dreamt I was having a full-blown conversation with Josiah. I knew he was in Spirit in my dream. I was sitting in my work room in my red and gold chair, just as I do when I write or meditate or go live on Facebook. It was the exact setting. I was sitting in the chair, but also watching from behind. I could hear his voice. His voice was clear, just as I know it. We were conversing. I was asking him questions and he was answering me, although I am not sure of the conversation, I am sure of the energy of it. As the dream continued; A young boy entered my work room with a balloon! Now, it feels like we were in my workroom, yet we were also outside. The wall with my window that faces the back yard is gone, and I can see the tree I created for him in my backyard. My older son Jeremy was standing in the room on my right. Witnessing everything. When the young boy entered my dream, it startled me! I began to tell Josiah what was going on, that a young boy just came in with a balloon and startled me! I was telling him this, like we were chatting on the telephone! Then I felt his energy! His spirit entered my body from the left and blended with mine! I could see it! I saw him to the left of me, and then I saw his energy blend into mine! The dream was cut short when someone knocked on our hotel door. It was five in the morning. Then I heard a knock on the door across the hall. Then on another door, and another and then back on our door. I jumped out of bed, startled and miffed that someone had woken me from my dream. No one was there, and there had been no voices. It woke Skylinn, my granddaughter. I asked her, "Did you hear knocking?" she whispered, "Yes!" and tumbled back into her slumber. I was wide-eyed. My mind filling with the memory of my dream, along with every sensation. I had heard him! I had felt him! He had blended with me! He had shown me how we can connect on even a deeper level. I quickly grabbed pen and paper, and huddled in the bathroom, and wrote every bit of this memory down, and dreamed of dreaming! But who was knocking?

The room was finally arising, and Valerie confirmed she had heard the knock also. We headed to breakfast where I teasingly told my sister I needed to speak to the management about the knocking. (She is the management.) She said it must have been kids. Kids? Wouldn't I have heard footsteps if there were kids! Wouldn't I have heard tiny voices? There were none. Only knocking. I outlined the story in my mind and clarity came. Josiah had knocked and woken me. Why? I was so happy in my dream. Why would he knock? Then I thought, why wouldn't he! *"Wake up mom! Write it down. And let the girls know I was here"*

California Adventure

I purposed in my heart that if the parade of dreams were passing by or anything that would tear my heart apart, I was going to avoid it. No need to terrorize the kids with my grief at Disneyland. This day was theirs, and it was obvious Josiah was with us! He always is, so why would I doubt it! But, just in case I had any question, he was going to throw in a couple more signs.

The day was early. I closed my eyes tightly as the Incredicoaster turned in a complete circle and the kids screamed with joy. Oh how I am not the roller coaster rebel of yesteryear. Now on to the sliding Pixar pal. The swinging Ferris wheel. This is the ride that was going to cultivate the most déjà vu for me. When I took the kids, Valerie was completely panicked on this ride. This Ferris wheel is huge. They escort you into a caged compartment with no seat belts to secure your body from sliding, as this enormous Ferris wheel goes around sliding down what looks like a thin pole, scaring the bejeezus out of you! Valerie was in a panic, and Josiah and I rocked that cage and made her cry. Not sad tears, just panicky, laughing tears. And since I too, am not a fan of heights, being in cahoots with Josiah to spook his sister, turned my own fears to laughter. In truth, we were all in panicky, laughing tears. This time around, Valerie overdramatized her fears, just to trick her kids, and make them laugh, which looped with my déjà vu, and granted my new memories to curl inside the old.

We continued to the next ride. One of our favorites, Soarin' Around the World. When we came years prior, this ride was called Soarin' over California. The ride lifts you up to witness a giant screen, creating a feeling like you are parasailing over California, adding the scents of ocean and orange blossoms. And now it's the world, with added scents of dirt and rain and more. Truly a remarkable ride. But what was even more remarkable was Josiah showing up again! There are thousands upon thousands of people at these parks. This line alone had to have had three hundred people in it, if not more. We walked through the maze ropes, until we were stopped by the hundreds of people in front of us, and socked in by the hundreds that followed. You really must make peace when you are in a line at a theme park, that waiting, is part of the fun. And the best part of waiting is getting to know the people that create this new circle you are now part of. Before we had the opportunity to meet our new neighbors, a young mother shouted out, "Josiah!"

By now Valerie was clearly aware her brother was beyond present, but come on now! Of all the thousands of people we could be standing next to in this parade of people, we were next to "Josiah!"

Valerie looked at me and said, "Don't say anything Mom, it will be weird!"

I am sure she thought if I spoke my truth, I would instantaneously drown from my tears, which would have been weird for this poor mother! We had a good forty-five minutes to play with Josiah. Never did we mention he was in Spirit and I think he appreciated that! Valerie only told her we had her little boy's name tattooed on us, and that her brother's name is Josiah too. There is something healing when you can acknowledge your child, or brother, and not have the need to share the pain. Skylinn and I decided on one ride, Seth and Valerie decided on another, so we went separate directions. At 2:22pm, Valerie texted me 222, letting me know she was in sync with her brother. I opened the text and as I was reading it, a tiny white butterfly passed over my phone, just like the mountain ceremony with Patricia.

"Son, I love you so much. I knew you would be here with us. You have superseded my wildest imagination. Don't ever stop!"

For Someone

I came back from that experience even more connected to the realm I am headed into. Ready to write. The weather shifted once more, and the rain came again. The words began to flow. Water tends to inspire me; it is a conductor. I get the biggest messages when I am in the shower. You know, the time where you cannot actually write, but your mind is ablaze with creative inspiration.

I dug into my book with a new fervency, my fears dropped, inspiration came. I just wanted to write. I understood from a new level what was next for me and where I was to go here on planet Earth, and in the ethereal with him. Earth and Spirit energy combined in one. I never really felt I was writing a story about Josiah or myself, it has always felt like I was writing to you, and for you, and about you. I am not writing a story about anything; I am writing a story for something. For someone. For you. I connected in with other mothers. I listened and read so many stories, anything that made me doubt myself was gone. Our lives are bigger than all of us.

I have shared many stories of waking up to words, images and information. These three happened within days of each other in early October. Just a mere two weeks before the one year. At the time of these bizarre awakenings, I was not particularly clear on what he was trying to tell me. Now I am coming into focus.

Heart~Soul~Spirit
ONE

I awakened to hear, *Heart, Soul, Spirit.*

"Wow! That is beautiful, baby!" I said, immediately knowing there was more. I poured myself a cup of coffee. "First things first, babe!" I opened my computer and googled, Heart, Soul, Spirit. And right there an image appeared with those three words and his necklace emblem behind it. The Tristeles!

I gasped, "How magic are you? You are blowing my mind again!" In a hush of knowing, I could hear him tell me, *"You are not a Mind, Body, Spirit Practitioner; you are a Heart, Soul, Spirit Practitioner!"* I really did not need to argue this information, since the words he was gracing me with were so beautiful, and clearly connected to his energy! I grabbed the picture off the internet and added it as my picture in my private Facebook group, retitled myself and continued on with my day in a rush of awe!

TWO

Grief bonder!

"What? What in the world is a grief bonder? Same dance: coffee, computer, google, grief bonder.

What pops up is continuing bonds; *The phrase "continuing bonds" was first used in 1996 to refer to an aspect of bereavement process in the title of the book, Continuing Bonds: Another View of Grief, which challenged the popular model of grief requiring the bereaved to "let go" of or detach from the deceased. It was clear from the data presented that the bereaved maintain a link with the deceased that leads to the construction of a new relationship with him or her. This relationship continues and changes over time, typically providing the bereaved with comfort and solace. Most mourners struggle with their need to find a place for the deceased in their lives and are often embarrassed to talk about it, afraid of being seen as having something wrong with them.*

"What am I reading right now?" I ask myself, and my

son. "I believe this wholeheartedly, that I have created this with you, we have a continuing bond. But why are you showing me this? I am not a grief bonder."

"Oh, but you are! Your message is that, our bonds continue! And there is nothing wrong with you for believing this, it is quite the opposite."

Josiah was right. We have the ability to continue our journey with our children, or anyone in Spirit. Yes, it is different, yes, it is still painful. It hurts. It sucks. But I would rather have these glistening majestic moments with him in Spirit, than not! The more I see, hear, and feel, the stronger the connection gets and the clearer he can come through. He sees from a perspective I cannot! I want his perspective! I always have!

THREE

Raina's Teaching.

My brain took quite a tumble at this one. Why I decided upon waking to look at Pinterest is beyond me. I had been looking for paint colors, and bathroom decorations, earlier in the year. Maybe I got a notification and it led me down that rabbit hole? Who knows? What I do know, is as I opened Pinterest, there it was! A spiritual quote and the words, "Raina's Teachings!" I had never seen this before. I had never even looked for spiritual quotes on Pinterest before! I scrolled more. There is another, and another. There are dozens of them.

I think, *What have I done in my sleep?* knowing it was nothing. I follow the link to the actual website of this Raina's teachings. At first glance, her logo looks exactly like the tree of life woman on my business logo! This morning there was no need for coffee. My heart was racing. What in the world? Come to find out in my diggings, that there is a woman who channels Raina, and these are her teachings! How did that end up on my Pinterest feed?

Heart, Soul, Spirit. Grief bonder. Raina's teaching. A complete message from Josiah, telling me to share my heart, soul, and spirit. Teach. And share that our bonds continue. Wow, just wow, babe!

Ladder Canyon

Early in 2019, Aimee and Jeremy decided it was time for family hikes. Our first hike was to ladder canyon. A unique hike out past Mecca California. There are multiple ladders strategically placed within the canyon making it possible for you to get to your next trail. Some are steep and kind of scary. It is a 4.5-mile hike, and on this particular day the skies were clear. The weather mild, with not a lot of wildlife or birds to speak of. On the way down through the canyon, you are greeted with giant rocks layered with quartz and silver.

I was walking ahead of Aimee when the intensity of her voice caught my ears. "Raina! Josiah!"

I turned to see a gigantic butterfly sailing towards me, weaving its way through us. There had not been one butterfly flying, nor any animal sightings, in the more than two hours we had been hiking. Then, in the vastness of the crystal cathedrals around us, came a butterfly!

The Cruise, 2019

It had been seventeen months since I'd gone anywhere with my husband, other than the store, a walk, or out to eat. I was still uneasy being far away from home, the house and my kids. I guess I would call this PTSD. Indeed, "disorder" is the perfect word to describe my life. I had Jeremy, Valerie and then Josiah. That is the order, and I am powerless to reclaim it. My emotional ability to wander off for a vacation, and experience life, had been muted. Being home was safe. Even pondering traveling with my friends left my mind circling. As my mother would say, "God forbid anything should happen!" There is truth in that quote. I had been gone the weekend of Josiah's exit! I had been so busy; I had been unable to talk with him. There was no way I could be that far from my other children, and grandchildren. Oh, they could run amuck! But I remained tethered to the safety of my house, just in case!

Poor Rich. Several times a week he would call me over to the computer to have me look at this place or that place to go. Some were just an hour away, others – including his number one choice, a cruise – would take us to other states and countries. My answer was always the same, "Yes, that does look nice, but no, not yet." He was always careful not to show his disappointment, that he was still unable to pry me from my comfort zone.

Medium/Mystic

In early February, I did wrestle my way to San Diego to attend a mediumship course with my friend Carolan. Our teacher was Andy Byng, with whom I had already taken several online classes. Andy has a gentle, straightforward way of teaching that both intrigued and nurtured me. My mission, of course, was to get closer to Josiah and hopefully strengthen my connection with Spirit in general. It may sound contradictory here, but I viewed this trip as completely different from going on a vacation (I know, poor Rich!) During our class, students would partner for a psychic or medium mystic assignment.

For our first task, which was to read each other's soul from a psychic perspective, I partnered with Lisa. She read me like she knew me, until she said something about seeing me at the ocean. "Did I like to go to the ocean?" she asked, to which I replied, "Everybody loves the ocean, but I am more of a mountain and lake kind of girl!"

"Hum. Well, I see you near the ocean." she said, confident about what she had seen. Later that morning I partnered with Angel, who, ironically, was Lisa's husband. I read him and then he began to read me. He was describing me exactly as his wife had, and as we had not had a break between exercises there was no way they could have conversed about me. I was so impressed how beautifully in sync they were, and then he said it: "I see you by the ocean. What's with the ocean and you?"

What the heck? Are you serious right now? I echoed what I had told Lisa, adding how blown away I was of their unique bond, and then it hit me.

"Well, my husband is constantly trying to get me to take a cruise."

"That's it, Raina!" Angel warmly smiled. "You should definitely take a cruise!" We laughed as I replied, "I guess I better."

Within days of my return home, Richard called me to look at yet another cruise, this one in April, when we had absolutely nothing going on. It left San Diego, went down into Mexico and back to San Diego. No flying and ridiculously affordable. "What do you think?" he asked hopefully yet no doubt anticipating a no.

"Okay," was all I said.

"Okay?" His brows raised like he had heard a foreign language!

"Yes, okay!"

I am not sure if I have ever seen him respond to anything so quickly. In minutes the trip was booked, and there was no turning back. I had to go to *the ocean!*

In truth, it was nice to get away. It surprised me that I was excited about it. And my poor neglected partner was, I am sure, happy to see a glimmer of joy in me and appreciative of the adventure. The yes had come easily this time, but I now had to hold back my feeling of being disloyal to my grief. I called Jeremy and guiltily told him we would be gone for a week in April. I suspected he might think I should be home too, but then he cheerfully said, "Good, Mom, you should go out and have some fun!" relieving me from a portion of my guilt, and nurturing the part of his mother that desperately needed to hear that.

Cabo

I did well while we stayed on the ship for the two days of cruising the open waters that Josiah had loved so much. I took my phone off airplane mode at the first port and the notices began to chime in. And there he was! The first notification was a picture I had taken, six years prior on this day, of Josiah wearing a psychedelic bandana. It was one of my favorite pictures of his warm smile. Sign One. I will take it! What are the chances? You cannot make this stuff up, and must believe that our Spirit team has lined up our kismet connections for us. The Alchemy of Josiah had proven so unique since day one. Why would I doubt this? "Send me a butterfly, babe!" Poor kid, I am never satisfied! Rich and I walked around the unique town of Cabo San Lucas until we reached the shore, lined with hotels, restaurants and parties. I stood there looking at the turquoise waters when my broken heart cracked through. My eyes began to well. "I love you Josiah!" I silently lamented, as a yellow butterfly came from the right of me, like it had been birthed from the ocean herself. It fluttered, crossing my face and then whished across the bay. "Josiah, was that you?" I heard him say, *"If that is not good enough, here is another one,"* as a white butterfly did the same dance.

All of a sudden, my heart felt lighter! The crashing waves chuckling for him in a way I could hear, *"You're ridiculous, Mom!"* I stepped onto the warm sand and told him, "I know, I'll see you soon!"

Oh, the silent tears I cry; they have become a part of me, drawn back to where they try to escape from.

Mazatlán

The early morning knock at my cabin door, announcing creamy coffee, startled me out of my dream. Another vivid dream in my awareness of no recall! Resting the warm cup against my aching abdomen, I began to meditate, asking Josiah to show himself to me once more, this time in Mazatlán. This day, we were to take a bus tour of the town. We would see the cliff jumpers, then take another transport boat to Stone Island for some playtime. I was, as always, looking for Josiah. The first sign came in the form of our guide, David. Josiah's middle name, "Hello Son." We hopped on the bus with ten other strangers, soon to be friends. The old town of Mazatlán is rich with history, culture, churches and open markets that carry meat and pig heads nuzzled next to clothes, and trinkets. The pig head was an extraordinary, smelly treat when I noticed J.E. tattooed on its forehead! Yes, this could be Josiah Elkins, but Josiah was a strict vegan so there is no way he was showing up in pig form. This was for Jeremy, my hunter-gatherer. I could say it was from Josiah for Jeremy, but I might be stretching with that one. We gathered back at the van and headed to the cliff side streets, where venders sold their goods, and cliff jumpers performed to our amazement. We had made two stops and seen much. But nothing stopped me more in my tracks than on our third stop. We all piled back into our seats; David put the van in reverse. I loomed out the window as the license plate next to us came into view and disappeared before I could snap a picture. I saw a JA-22, (Josiah Akoya 22), then we turned away. But I know what I saw. I quickly wrote it down as David headed to our tour boat, which would take us to Stone island.

There, on the mini cruise, I would have another moment with Josiah. We had crossed the waters and were pulling into the dock when I was suddenly overcome with emotions. I have learned over the months that this intensity means Josiah is near. I turned my body to face the ocean behind us so no one, especially Rich, would see me shed my tears. He was so excited about Stone Island I just could not let him see me cry. And, anyway, this was my moment alone. Facing the back of the boat, I felt that guilty grief all over again. "Why do I get to be here, and he does not? I should have stayed home!" Suddenly, over to the left of the boat, a flock of birds began to dance and sing in theatrical unison. I thought "No!", then heard "Yes!" *Really? Josiah? Am I just making this stuff up?* When the boat attendant snapped me out of it telling me we were here, I looked at this jovial young man and said, "Your name?"

"José, ma'am." Now I know José is a popular Spanish name, but come on – José and David?"

Puerto Vallarta

The following day there was no agenda. Just letting the breeze take us at its will. We headed downtown to old Puerto Vallarta. I was fascinated with the cobblestone streets, greenery and the mysterious art and magic this town had. We walked for miles, taking in the eye candy and spiritual energy. I felt charged. We found the pier with water taxis that could take us to the island of

Yelapa, but it was leaving in five minutes! We rushed back off the pier to the tiny office where we could buy tickets. The clerk helped us and escorted us hurriedly back to the taxi just in time to jump onto the boat. Rich handed me our handwritten ticket to put in the backpack. Like a beam shooting out the page was the clerk's name – David! – and I sensed we were headed to the right destination.

Yelapa is the coolest town, with streets only wide enough for an ATV. I was captivated. When was I going to move here? I could see me living here for months, writing and painting and receiving. I could also see Josiah being here in this bohemian spirit that possessed this place. I felt reassured and reawakened in the small jungle atmosphere I was privileged to be in.

We walked up the steep condensed streets to the waterfall that graced the top of this city. Hundreds of butterflies flickered around me, like fairies, in this fairytale I had become part of. We descended through the town, and homes, that lined the tiny street, to the tourist beachfront that would rest my soul for the next few hours. It felt good to do nothing!

As peaceful as the quiet can be, it is also reflective. I was one week into my "Double 30s" (I'd just turned sixty) and this quiet spot has my heart stirring. The feeling of that moment when I called that hospital, hundreds of miles away, broke my silence and began to crackle through the calm I was longing for. I was then taken back to my birthday. My sister and Rich took me to Cirque du Soleil. Richard daring to buy the tickets, knowing this was something Josiah and I loved doing together. I had that guttural feeling when he told me he had a surprise for me. I just knew. He walked up to me on my birthday with an envelope in hand.

"Want to know what your surprise is?"

I looked at him through my mascara layered lashes. "I know what it is, Cirque. You are taking me to see Cirque du Soleil!" Puzzled, but really not that surprised, that I knew, he handed me the tickets. I handed him a picture of Josiah at one of our Cirque's dates. I had already dug it up to take with me. I was nervous and apprehensive. I did not think this was a good idea at all. Could I even handle this? We walked up to the big semi that had the picture of the cast of characters on it. I took out Josiah's picture, and Rich turned photographer, proceeded to take as many pictures as I wanted.

In the theater, I was slightly on edge, waiting for the performance that might send me to the loony bin. And then it happened. My emotional response was over-whelming. The rush of tears streamed down my face and through the veins of my soul. I thought the audience may turn, and pierce me with their glares for disturbing them with my anguish. One by one, the round halos, called the Cyr Wheel, that had become Josiah's signature act, rolled onto the stage. Six, possibly eight of them. Emotions rendered me incapable of counting. They began to spin the ballet of the Cyr Wheel. Each spin clutched around my heart, like a hand squeezing it. Then the next one started to spin, layered with another hand. And then another and another until I busted from compression. I forced myself to regain my composure. I told myself, "He did not perform with others. He was a solo act. This was different. Look at it. It is beautiful. See the beauty. Josiah would see this and rejoice in the magic they are giving you. *He* is giving you!"

I pulled my attention back to the present moment. To the beach front and the ocean.

I sat there staring at the ocean and musing how I often used it to describe myself when people asked how I was doing. "I am an ocean, it comes in waves!" Later that evening as I looked over the ocean, I saw the truth of the wave. I could hear Yanni playing in the background. Yanni used to lull my children to sleep, back when it was just me and them. Chills consumed me as Josiah came close; my eyes started to fill and I said, "Josiah, I am an ocean, you are the waves!" These are the waves of love I have come to embrace. The waves of love that fill me with so much pain it can only be felt *because* I love.

Fiddler on the Roof

Back home and somewhat rested, I was convinced that my son travels with me always. No matter where I go, there he will be. I felt a bit more capable of wandering, even though I was in no hurry to go anywhere. I had Mother's Day upon me once again. I had scheduled to go see Jaye on May 8th but couldn't land on what I would want tattooed on me this time. I was unsure if I should cancel. What am I going to do on May 8th, if I do not get this annual tattoo that I'd thought would ease the day's pain? Checking my email, I see that *Fiddler on the Roof* was playing in Orange County, near Sheri's house. *Fiddler on the Roof* was all about my parents. We know all the songs by heart because they would sing to us the songs from the movie. And how timely, since our father had left this earth on May 11th. I forwarded the email to Sheri in hopes she would be free to go with me. She responded quickly, with a "Yes, let's go!" The dates that were open were May 7th and May 8th. I allowed the Universe to step in, told her my tattoo dilemma, and to get the seats that were best. They were on the 8th which sealed the date and answered my question. It was not time for a tattoo! Our parents wanted us with them. But I still desperately needed my son.

Sheri had suggested we go to a vegan restaurant near our venue to honor Josiah. As we pulled into the parking lot, I was immediately taken years back. Josiah and I had come here. He had taken me to a shop here, to show me something he wanted for his birthday. We wandered the shops and ate at this restaurant that Sheri was now taking me to. We ordered a vegan pastrami for our parents and headed to the venue, crying like babies through the entire performance. The actors were as good, if not better, than those in the movie. I knew we were where we were supposed to be.

Siobhan

I was about to encounter Josiah in a big way, and I think he already knew this. The following Saturday I had a reading set up with a medium named Siobhan. She lives in London and knew nothing about me. This would be my first reading from someone who did not know me. I sat in my room and wrote Josiah before signing into Zoom for my appointment.

> *Josiah,*
>
> *I need you to come through today. I just need an additional expression of you. A confirmation, guidance. I know you are here; I know that I know, but could you please intermingle with Siobhan, and let me hear you from this perspective too!*
>
> *Yes. Your answer is always yes to me. Always. You are standing right next to me. Holding space for my heart to rest. Guiding my world and my hand, as it graces the keyboard. Help me son. Help me to be your extension.*

I patiently waited for Siobhan. She started the reading by telling me she had already tuned in and had written some things down. She asked me if my son was in Spirit. When I told her yes, she asked, "Was there cancer?"

When I told her yes, she added, "But that is not how he crossed. He was a faith healer."

My jaw dropped.

"You and he are alike," she said, "You are a faith healer!"

"Yes!"

"You are both natural healers. He was a true lightworker."

"Yes!" I felt I had no other words.

"Who is Anne?" she asked.

"My grandmother was Anna, and my daughter's middle name is Anne."

"Your daughter, she is open to her brother?"

"Yes!"

"Good," she told me. "He watches over her!"

Siobhan was not the first one to tell me this, and I knew it to be true.

On a Friday night a couple of months earlier, Valerie was in her own personal dilemma. She kept texting me evidence that her brother was with her that night! They'd had Chinese for dinner, and she found a 22 on her fortune cookie read out. Dimes in random places. Even her son Seth was finding dimes! I told Josiah that I was glad he was with Valerie, but he lived with me, and needed to come home that night. Yes, I really said that! And you know what? He did. I fell asleep on the couch and was jolted awake at 10:22 p.m.! I looked at the clock, knowing he had woken me. "I am glad you are home, thank you for waking me to let me know, I love you!"

Siobhan went on. "I wrote October and the number 19?"

"He left in October, and his birthday is August 19th."

"You two are soulmates!" I had heard that a couple of times as well and, given that I thought he has been my dad, and the ancestry meaning I got early on, it made sense. She read my soul and where she thought I may go from here. Then she said, "You are doing something big, something about his legacy. Are you writing a book?"

"Yes!"

She then asked the significance of the year 1988.

"The year he was born!" I exclaimed. I was impressed for sure. "Something with his left toe? Or left foot? It is permanent. Did he hurt his left foot? Does he have a scar there?" Josiah had hurt his foot in high school while climbing up the Del Taco flagpole like a monkey, but I couldn't remember if it was his left or right foot; also, there had been no permanent issue. Then I looked across my room, and there, peering out from behind a book, was Josiah's left baby footprint! I had placed it behind the book on the bookshelf for safe keeping. It was the tattoo I had been considering! If that is not permanent, I don't know what is.

"Siobhan!" I exclaimed, "Look!" I picked up my computer and turned it around so she could see the footprint.

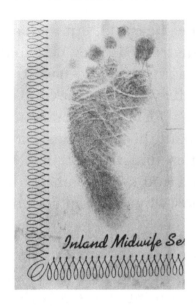

Inland Midwife Se

Then, just when I was sure it couldn't get better she told me that Josiah influences my cat. I had not told her I had a cat, and I knew she was right about that.

Then she said, "Purple. Your aura is purple, or violet, and so is Josiah's!" Again, I jumped up to show her my purple tank top and tie-dyed leggings. I had reasons for my purple display.

"Siobhan, this morning I had on a burgundy tank with black leggings, when something told me to change into purple! I literally said out loud, "I think I need to wear purple!" I changed and then told Josiah, "I feel like I have to dress for you." and by the way, my cat's name is Violet!" We talked a bit more. Her comments about the feet and the color purple had blown my mind. I was utterly amazed.

I took Josiah's baby footprints from the bookshelf and sent a picture to Jaye. "Can you tattoo this?"

She told me she could, but then a few days later she wrote to me, distressed. They had sold the building her tattoo shop was in and she had to relocate. She was crushed that she would not be able to salvage the elfin cement benches Josiah had constructed for her. I knew how she felt about those benches, but I also knew Jaye's creative abilities and trusted that she would salvage what she could and create something that held Josiah in it. Now I knew why I had not gotten that Mother's Day tattoo.

"Jaye when you get moved, I will come and have Josiah's footprints done in the new shop. I am guessing he wants his footprints there too!

Sedona, 2019

June was pleasantly disrupted by a message from my friend Michelle, saying she had a gift for me. Surprised and thrilled that she had thought of me, I asked if she wanted to connect the following day. She said that wouldn't work, as she was heading to Sedona early in the morning. Could she come now?

At the time, I had my hands full, making sandwiches for my grandchildren who were gathered around the kitchen island, but I couldn't help but wonder what was so pressing that she had to come right away. Of course, I told her.

The sandwich feast commenced, and I had just enough time to clean the kitchen before Michelle arrived. Jeremy had picked up Gavin for a dentist appointment, and I settled the others in to watch a movie as Michelle and I chatted. She told me her trip to Sedona would be a solo one, which I found interesting and, truth be told, was slightly envious of. Venturing off by myself had been a wish of mine, and more prominent since Josiah's birthday. I had brushed it back from the forefront, questioning whether the wish was for healing, or simply to run away.

"Michelle. I am so jealous. If I would have known, I would have gone with you."

"Really?" she said, saying she had announced it on social media, but no one had said they could go.

"I did not see that, I wish I had!" We went round and round about how I wished I had seen it, and how she wished I had too, finally concluding we would plan something in the future. Then off she went, leaving me to gawk over my gift. A tasseled black backpack she said, "had Raina written all over it!"

Rich came home shortly afterward. When I told him of our conversation, and my wish that I had known about Sedona, he replied, "Go."

"What?"

"Just go with her." Hearing his words, I realized how my spontaneous energy had been buried, not only by Josiah's leaving, but the years of fear and uncertainty, due to his illness, that preceded it. "What do you have going on this weekend that you can't reschedule?"

I opened the calendar app on my phone. "Nothing," I said, "I have absolutely nothing going on this weekend." I paused, my need to stay close to home resurfacing, "but I think she wants to go alone."

"Just ask her. If she wants to go alone she will tell you." Oh, my wise Guru! I messaged Michelle, who responded immediately. "Yes, come, I would love that, I will pick you up in the morning!"

I gathered the grandkids and drove to Brian's house, our meeting place for our Thursday evening family hikes. As we drove up, I saw Jeremy's car and the excitement hit me. I opened the gate, barely able to contain myself.

"Jeremy, guess what happened between the time you picked up Gavin and now?"

He looked over from the BBQ. "What?"

"I am going to Sedona!"

He was thrilled that I was getting away; he could also see that beneath my excitement, I still had reservations, "Mom, it's okay. Go live your life. Everything will be okay. You deserve to have fun and be happy!"

The next morning, at 6:44, Michelle and I ventured out. As we turned the corner of the street a bunny crossed our path. Little did we realize that this was the first of the "little spirit teachers," as Native Americans describe animals, that were going to guide us along our way. Rabbits in particular teach us about personal transformation, "hopping to it," and stepping into the abundance of creativity we have within us.

We arrived in Quartzsite, "wow!" was reverberating between us as we saw the clock: 9:44 a.m. There was one lonely Rock Shop opened, and we were headed in. If you are anything like me, hours can go by in a crystal store, and you have not even made it halfway through. Those shiny, and non-shiny gems hold stories of their own. Which story are you supposed to take home with you, keeps you looking! Back in the car, we were examining our matching sister stones when the clock spoke again, 11:44am. Both amazed, we drove towards Sedona. The sequential numbers continued the entire trip. In the car at 11:11 a.m., out at 1:11 p.m. In at 10:33 a.m., out at 11:33 a.m. This continued the entire trip, along with our animal totems.

When we arrived in Sedona, Michelle had already chosen a vegetarian restaurant she had found on the internet. The ChocolaTree. Sounded perfect to me. I walked into the restaurant and lost my breath. Everything I laid my eyes upon resonated with somewhere I had been with Josiah. It was part health food store, vegan bakery and restaurant. Artwork for sale was sprinkled throughout as we walked through the narrow hallway to the bohemian outdoor seating. We sat to the back so we could look forward and take it all in. There was just a hint of a breeze blowing. A tiny leaf, no bigger than my thumbnail landed on the table.

"Michelle, look it's a heart!" I said, pointing to the tiny leaf that had fallen from the sky the moment I sat down at the table. We were then visited by an orange-breasted bird. It was an American Robin, and I knew Josiah had influenced the beautiful bird to sit beside us. I looked up what this bird could represent. *"This bird teaches you how to incorporate new beginnings, trusting in the process. It reminds you to believe in yourself and to use the inspiration that is given. To Listen carefully and sing your own song for a new period in your life."* My son has been asserting this message on me since day one, and it was clear, he was not letting up on me, or Michelle! We headed to the hotel, and the numbers that surrounded us at every corner spoke volumes.

Our next visitor was a Blue Jay. We had taken a jeep tour to the spiritual sights and vortexes that is the lace Sedona is weaved upon. Our tour guide, Patrick, a like-minded man and a fast friend, knew exactly what we wanted and made sure we had the experience we longed for. We visited the Amitabha Stupa and Peace Park. As we were about to leave, a bird appeared. We quietly stood by to see if this was a visitation or just a quick hello. The bird stayed still, peering at us. We took in its glory until it told us we could go. We continued to the hilltops of the energy vortex, listening to the familiar language of the wind.

We had just gotten back in the jeep to head to our last stop when out of nowhere, a Red Cardinal flew across the road in front of us. Michelle's head boomeranged back toward me, and as she began to speak, Patrick's voice blended with hers.

"Raina! A red cardinal, do you know what that means?"

"Yes!" I exclaimed. Red Cardinals hold many spiritual meanings and have long been seen as messengers from heaven.

"Red cardinals," Patrick said with awe in his voice, "are rare here in Sedona. In fact I have never seen a red cardinal the entire time I have lived here!"

Red cardinals are not in southern California either, so I too had never seen one. *That was profound, Josiah!*

When we got back to the hotel, I googled Blue Jay and was once again blown away.

Call on blue jay spirit when you need to be powerful, or stand in your own power...when you need to be confident, or stand in your own confidence... when you need to move to the next level of your life or begin again... when you need to fulfill the desires of your heart. (These were the same messages rabbit and robin had been saying.) And the most important message for me: *When you need to understand death!*

There in the abyss, we call a cell phone, I was reading words that confirmed these signs that were happening all around us. We had one more animal visitor that night as we set out to visit the night sky and watch the stars flicker. This time it was a four-legged friend: a coyote.

Coyote symbolism is reminding you to laugh at yourself. Things have been entirely too serious of late. Therefore, you simply need to let loose and get on with it. Coyote symbolism insists that you stop dwelling on your worries and stresses and let them go. Furthermore, since you have asked for the help, you must get out of the way of yourself. Let go and allow your spirit helpers to do what they need to do. Coyote meaning is signaling you to do something that gives you pleasure and joy and focus on the positive for a change. Live in the present moment, find joy in all of the things they do.

As we laid on the ground watching the glittered sky above us, I reflected on how fascinating this journey had been. All our messengers aligned; every day starting and ending in numerical sequences. We had met the most interesting people, one whose father lived in our hometown. And then there were the dreams that woke me from my slumber. Josiah filled my senses.

"Mom, I am in all of this, everywhere you look, I am!"

I nodded in knowing, as the rush of truth swept through me. My spell was then disrupted by the roar of an engine coming upon us. I reached out to Michelle, who was closer to the road and yelled, "Get up!"

Nearly in hysterics, we jumped to our feet, only to realize we were nowhere near getting run over by the motorhome that zipped by. The rush of adrenaline from the prospect of it was worth the momentary fright. This time it was tears of unexplainable laughter that filled our faces. We took to another area where we were less likely to be run over, to view our stars. This time, when the coyote appeared again, we were doing something we loved, and joy had filled our perceptions.

The next morning, we got up early, packed and headed out for our final quest: a hike deep into the red dirt mountain trail near the Cathedral. Walking this path takes you to what feels like another planet, where the mountain takes on forms that resemble cruise ships, spaceships, and other formations you can decide what you see in them. We stopped to overlook the valley. The breeze of silence surrounded us. Michelle's voice was calm and quiet as she spoke.

"I think Josiah is really happy you are here. He just wants you happy and to release your worries."

My eyes welled in acknowledgement as his voice echoed her words in my heart. We took in the beauty that surrounded us. *"Mom, I am in everything you see!"*

he reminded me. We collected rocks and started our voyage home. Although we were in no hurry, Michelle decided to see how many miles it was to home from where we were. It was 555! "Hello Spirit!"

The clock continued to speak through numbers each time we stopped on the way home. As we turned the corner to my street and Michelle's tires landed on my driveway, the car was no longer in possession of the clock, Josiah was. By now, Michelle was clearly aware of his signature, 22, and his deep love that comes at 10:22. The clock read, 10:22 pm. The song on her radio, "Don't worry, Be Happy!" The exact words Michelle had quietly spoke over me that morning. We sat in the car blown away, speechless over the magnitude of Josiah's ability to communicate with us. The next morning, I was unpacking my backpack and at the bottom of the backpack was... a dime!

Camping, July 2019

On our second day in the Sierra mountains, I sat on the shore at Silver Lake writing and watching my grand-kids, Richard, Jeremy, Aimee and Michael out on the lake fishing. Already Josiah's presence was unmistakable, and I had to document it. While packing to come up to the Sierras, I was listening to medium Laura Lynne Jackson's new book, *Signs*. I heard her say, "Chapter 22: Camouflage, a gun and a new as-signment," I listened to the chapter in awe. Both my husband and Jeremy are camo men. Hunter-gatherers all the way, and I have definitely been put on a new assignment in this life! Was this another sign from Josiah? Chapter 23 was about "babies and bears"; I was on my way to the mountains with my babies! Camo and a gun and a new assignment? Chapter 22... coincidence? I think not, that is synchronicity. The night before I had fallen asleep while watching Grey's Anatomy. At the end of each episode there is always a summary of the life lesson they are trying to convey. I was startled awake in time to hear, "Don't ditz the Juju, wherever it may come from!" My eyes stuck to the clock's numbers, 10:22pm. I was being told to see everything as a sign, as if I needed a reminder! Just two days prior to that, my daughter flew to Illinois. I received a text from her: "We are leaving from Gate 22, Mom, and it's the Owl flight!"

Now, up here in the mountains at our campsite, we all hiked down the steep trail to Little Walker Lake, a ridiculous one-mile incline that wipes the breath out of you on the way back up. I swear, I thought Rich was trying to kill me the first time he took me here. I had to stop so many times, my heart beating so fast I thought it may burst. Before I even reach the bottom, my two grandsons, Seth and Blaze run up to me wide eyed and hearts racing.

"Seth fell down!" Blaze exclaimed.

"Yes," Seth added, "I slid down the hill and guess what happened?"

"Grandma!" they both exclaimed. "A butterfly circled us! A Butterfly! Josiah!" They then grabbed my arm to assist me the rest of the way while repeating the Josiah butterfly story again. As if this wasn't amazing enough, I had just seen what appeared to be that same butterfly, up that steep incline at the campsite a few minutes earlier.

Later that evening, we all sat sipping hot chocolate, and chatting about our day's events around the campfire when that same butterfly whirled through our family circle.

"Did you see that?" Blaze, Seth and I sang out to each other in synchronistic rhythm. The following morning, I had the opportunity to sit quietly alone and sip my morning coffee while being entertained by the chipmunks. One was very attentive to me, so I walked closer to check it out. This busy chipmunk just stayed put. Looking at me with an intense stare, as if it were trying to tell me something. Later I was cleaning out the tent and I found a dime. A dime on the floor of the tent? A dime? Out in the middle of nowhere? Sunday morning, we drove up to Little Lake Virginia. I have wanted to show Jeremy this area for years. It is the most beautiful place in the Sierras, in my opinion. As we were driving the curvy road towards the lake, here he comes again in butterfly form, straight across the driver's side windshield of the truck.

"Rich, did you see?" Josiah is saying, "See what my mom sees, Rich!"

Rich smiled that half-grin smile, the one that says, "I know, and I believe, I just do not want to admit it!"

While paddle boating on Little Virginia that day, the seagulls had quite the performance for us, a ballet of songs they were singing, one to another. One in particular stayed close, and then started circling and sliding across our boat. I was hypnotized and unable to catch it on my camera, as it graced our presence. I asked Josiah to influence the bird one more time so I could catch its glory. He did, and I, like a crazy photographer, captured him in full flight! This was by far one of the most spectacular expressions of nature I had witnessed. We headed back to our campsite to pack it up and begin our five-hour ride home.

In the meantime, Valerie had been trying to get home from Illinois for two days now. Her flights had been delayed and changed by the airline. She had been stuck in the airport for hours and her nonstop flight, now had a full day layover in Denver. The silver lining: being able to spend the day with her high school bestie Bobbi. Still, she was fatigued and frustrated as we texted on my drive home, desperately wanting to be home herself. Then I get this message from her: "Boarding, I am in seat 22!" Gate 22 on departure, seat 22 on her final flight home.

"Oh, how he watches over his sister!" I replied to her as tears flooded my vision of the phone. We arrived home at 1:00 a.m. Jeremy's carload arrived at his house around three, the same time Valerie finally made it home. Monday, as Jeremy was walking home from our local sandwich shop, there on the sidewalk was a clear quartz crystal. Stunned, he sent me a picture of it. "Your brother is really trying to get your attention!" I replied. Tuesday, Richard went deep sea fishing out on the Pacific Ocean. When he came back that evening, he sent me a picture of his catch, and a military boat that was out in the waters beside him. "Look at the number on the boat!" It was 22.

"I told you," I replied, "Josiah really wants you to believe!"

Two Years

Two years was creeping in. Like a giant tidal wave in slow motion. I could see it in the distance, and I was scrambling for shelter.

I had made plans to go to a mediumship training on the 13th of October.

My need to press in and stay connected is never ceasing. The month before, I had gone to a weekend training with Apryl Nicole. During those three days Josiah was silent. So many others heard from their loved ones in Spirit, including my friend Suzanne, who I had traveled to this training with; her son had come through loud and clear the very first evening as we sat outside around the patio table in Joshua Tree. I kept my cool and was grateful this beautiful mother had received her message. The following day during our training, I waited. I asked Josiah repeatedly to come through someone, anyone! Nothing! The silence was deafening. "Why?" I asked him. Again, nothing. Later that day, Apryl questioned Suzanne and I: Were we related? Why were our energies so enmeshed?

This was interesting, as we were not sitting by each other at the time. I also had not told anyone there about Josiah. I had to come clean. "I also have a son in Spirit."

The room went still with surprise. Although Josiah did not make an appearance, Apryl understood the intensity of Suzanne's and my relationship. As the training ended, there was still no message from Josiah, at least not from the other mediums. Then he spoke in my ear, quietly, almost in a whisper. *"Mom, this was for you to learn. If I had spoken, that would have been all you thought about. You know I am here."*

As much as I did not like this, I could accept it. He was right. I could come to a place of understanding that he had stepped back in order for me to step forward. Then, in the one-day training in October, and the week to come, he was about to turn the tide of this wave and blow my mind like I have never experienced before.

The training was a reunion of sorts as I saw several of the people I'd made deep connections with at the previous training. Apryl started the day with psychic training, then moved on to mediumship after lunch. After announcing that she would demonstrate first, she scanned the room, feeling energetically the spot or person where she was being pulled. She spoke to one person, and then another, then she said she had a father. She went on to describe the father's energy, how he'd lived, and how he died. Suzanne was sitting next to me with her son's father, John. She nudged John and said, "That is your father!"

John spoke up, drawing Apryl's attention. She went on to talk of his father, then said she heard the name Taylor.

"Is that your son?" she asked, to which Suzanne and John said it was. After speaking of Taylor in detail, she said he had another young man with him, a young man with angelic energy. She said she heard the name, Messiah, but her voice had a question in it.

"Does that make sense to you?"

"Yes," Suzanne said, "Taylor had a friend in Spirit who was religious."

"Have you rediscovered your religion?" Apryl asked, "Because Messiah has to do with that, right? Connecting to your Messiah?" Then she paused again, with a questioning demeanor, and said, "No! I am hearing the name, Messiah!"

I blurted out, "Josiah!"

Apryl looked at me and said, "Josiah? I am not familiar with that name, that makes sense. Is this your son?"

"Yes" I blubbered.

"He is telling me that he left his body before anything happened. Does this make sense to you, because he is adamant! He is saying, 'Tell my mom, tell my mom, my spirit left before. My mom has to know this!'"

"Yes!" I said. Once again he was confirming what I knew.

"And do you understand a motorcycle?"

"Yes!" I held my tears right at the rim of my eyes.

"You know your son has a huge presence!"

"Yes!"

"And that he is doing big work on the other side!"

"Yes!"

"He says to get out of the labyrinth. He is not in there. He is on the other side. He says you are afraid you will not get there, but he wants you to know you will. He says, 'Who do you think taught me to get here? You did! And you will get here.' He is telling me to tell you to Reiki your ears so you can hear him better. He wants you to listen. And he is talking about the last dream he was in. He was trying to tell you something, does that make sense?"

"Yes! It does!"

"You need to be teaching, Raina, do you teach?"

"I do."

Then she paused and said, "Are you writing a book? He says to finish the book!"

It would take me a bit to unravel what had just happened. In the dream she was referring, Josiah had been watching me showing my guests the mementos in the small cabinet of my home. He had told me in the dream that, *"It was small."* I had told him my whole home is a sanctuary for him. Then when I had meditated on the dream, he gave me the clarity to understand that I was looking but not seeing. Was I hearing and not listening? Is that what he was trying to convey with the need to Reiki my ears?

The next morning, I had a disturbing phone call that left me frustrated. I did not understand why this was happening on the cusp of such an exceptional encounter with Josiah. I had to find peace. I walked out to my front yard where the three tall trees had housed butterfly Josiah, two distinct times since he left. Rich was watering the flowers. There were several smaller butterflies dancing around me. They seem to be waltzing with the water, when all of a sudden, the exact black and yellow butterfly I had witnessed in the first few days of his leaving appeared and settled in the middle tree, just as it had back then.

"Rich!" I exclaimed quietly, hopeful that the butterfly would remain. I stood, gazing upwards towards the leaves that now housed my son's butterfly energy.

"Look up, Mom, get out of the labyrinth. Nothing matters but this!" He was reminding me that I was looking sideways and taking my eyes off the spiritual lesson I was supposed to learn. As soon as I understood what he was saying, he flew towards me and away...

Luckily, the next few days were busy with clients and grandchildren. I think that maybe if I can just make it to the 22nd I will not be hit by the tidal wave I can clearly see suspended over me. But clients go home, and so do grandchildren. Eventually I knew the weight of the water was going to consume me. Saturday, I could feel my body slowing down, tired from the dog paddling I had been doing to keep my head above water. I was quieting and my breath was shallow. I just wanted to lay still and do nothing. So, I did.

Sunday, I forced myself to go out to my grief group. I looked at the wave above me and asked it to please stay back. What if we all let our waves crash together? That would be way too intense! Go in there and be brave instead of needing, I urged myself. Every one of the broken hearts before me were grappling with the hurt of anger, which paused me out from under the wave. I was angry too. That disturbing encounter had broken my heart, and I was angry about it. I was shocked that, this is what arrived, as the wave receded. My grief group is hosted by my friend AmyLynn. Her ability to guide us through our emotions with music therapy is always seamless. She had us using drums for this exercise. We were to choose a drum, play it, and then write what we had experienced. How it made us feel and/or think. Then we would choose another drum and do the same thing again. We did this four times, with four drums, each drumbeat representing a new thought. When we were done, we took a minute to analyze what we had written, and what came through. To my amazement, I was clear. I had released all my anger through the initial story I had shared with them. When I finally spoke it out loud, and without all the emotional details, I realized how ridiculous the whole thing was. I had been laughing as I told them, and each crackle allowed me to let go of what someone else's baggage is. I was not the holder of it, nor did I need to be. Josiah had told me to get out of the labyrinth swiftly, and I had. I thought I was going to go into that meeting completely consumed in grief, but how could I feel him if I have anger? That had to be removed before I could continue. I had learned a valuable lesson that week. Never ever will I allow another person to put a labyrinth before me, that is not of my choosing.

Monday, October 21, 2019

One more day until I hit this two-year mark, that still seems so unbelievable. I am lethargic. What am I going to do tomorrow? Just like his birthday in August, I feel this need to be alone. I am aimless, so why drag anyone else along aimlessly. I walk back and forth through the house, trying to figure out what to do today. It is not like I now have some magical ability to do anything that requires real focus anyway, and even if I did, that focus would bring tomorrow too quickly. I stay up just shy of midnight, as if maybe I can hold back the 22nd. Like that would truly change how I feel. Nothing will change this day or the next.

October 22, 2019

I wake up to the watchfulness of my husband. He is encouraging me to go work out with him. "It will make you feel better," he declares. Maybe he is right? Maybe circulating blood through my heart and brain, would be a good idea to help me navigate this day. I oblige. I walk into the gym, numb. Looking at each person, as they move their bodies with their personal rhythms. Not one person in here knows what day it is. I put my earbuds in to seclude myself from conversations. What could I possibly have to converse about to these innocent bystanders of my day?

Inside this pathetic attempt to work out, I decide to travel to Pioneertown. To Boulder Gardens. To see Josiah's dome home above the rock, that he had created. I had not been back to see it since he had lived there. I packed up some food and water and started my trek. First stop was to my friend Bonnie's. Bonnie is a crystal healer and had agreed to see me. I was in deep need of some healing, and I knew she would follow the lead of my needs.

Afterward, as I began to drive away from her house and head to the dome home, the time on my clock was the time Josiah ascended. I was shaken and started to cry and howl his name. I was just about to enter the freeway on ramp when I noticed that my odometer was at eighty-eight-something thousand miles. The year he was born. It made me smile, but not enough to stop me from enlightening Josiah how hard this was. Then another vehicle passed me, and the license plate had eighty-eight in it. I laughed and a new calm came over me. I stopped crying and another car went by with the same number in the license plate.

"Okay! Okay! You are here! I will drive calmly."

I had forgotten how far out the dome home was. Down a long windy road made of dirt and sand. When I arrived, I was greeted with heart-shaped cactuses and crystals surrounding the teepee Garth lives in. It was a quiet day out there. Garth and his friend were sitting around the outdoor kitchen table, talking and taking in the day. I introduced myself, not as Raina, but as Josiah's mom, and asked if I could visit the dome home.

"Of course," Garth said as he slid a stone inlaid pipe towards me and said, "Josiah made this for me." That made my heart so happy to know after all these years, he was using the gift Josiah had made him. I gathered my emotions from across the ethers and carried them all inside the dome, where I was expecting to unload them. The stairway up to the dome is decorated with mosaic tiles, that wrap around the giant stone towards the top. And a lone branch holds itself over the stairway, like a guard you must bow to in order to continue up the stairs. As I approached Josiah's wooden carved door, tears that had been suspended finally let loose. The door is magnificent, and opens to what they call, "The Cosmic Castle."

Everything inside was different, but the structure was the same. The shelves, the windows and Josiah's woodwork were magically perfect. I wrestled with the thought of becoming a thief and stealing all his woodwork to have as my own, but it was fleeting. I would never want to disturb the radiance he created. I sat in the core of the dome and soaked in every bit I could. I could hear the winds ferocious story. It was reminding me of the intensity of today. I looked around the space, hoping for a sign, when a dime caught my eye. A dime? Really? I had brought a picture of Josiah to accent his dome home, The Cosmic Castle. I took the frame, wrote all his qualities on the white matting.

I glued the dime on it and placed the picture I had brought in the frame and set it on an antique table that sat there waiting for it. The wind continued to force its attention on me. I said my goodbyes to Garth, the boulders, and to the Cosmic Castle that now had Josiah's face in it. I headed back through the sandy road, out toward the desert streets of Joshua Tree.

Could Jaye see me today? Jaye had just relocated

her tattoo shop. I had seen pictures and was eager to see her artistic creation in person. I walked in just as she had finished with her last client of the day.

"Good!" I told her as I preceded to show her pages and pages of Josiah's art, and the ideas that were swimming through my mind. I had brought his baby footprint but was not sure how I wanted that and where. What I was for sure about was wanting the exact tattoos Josiah had put behind his ears. He had spent some time designing, or shall I say channeling, the perfect frequencies, and meanings for these tattoos. One for the left ear and one for the right. The left symbol, "to receive and hear truth. Trust the divine flow of the Universe. Love unconditionally!" The right, "Allow wisdom to sing clearly. Hold clear, open and receptive to another. Expand patience!" This had to be on me. I needed these frequencies that were also on Josiah. I wanted teal for my left, this one was about truth and love, and teal is the perfect balance of green and blue, for the heart and throat chakra. Purple for my right, for the third eye and crown chakra. I felt complete and light when she was done. Like bliss had just filled me from within. I felt happy. Happy? I felt happy? Of all the days of the year, I had just done something so honorable for Josiah that I was happy, and it felt good! Now the hour drive home. Was this bliss going to last? Maybe! I had just created bliss!

Wednesday, Oct 23rd, 2019

I made it through the day, and I felt good about the way I had spent it. I was in "puzzling peace," a state I have come to understand when a layer of myself is re-structured. Before I had a moment to recall the previous day, I got a call that help was needed to take my grand-daughter to school. I was leaving the high school drop off zone when my phone lit up from Rain. We had been instant messaging all day yesterday, swearing we would never be without each other on his Ascension Day again. Was she okay? I couldn't wait to get home to find out, so I pulled over to read what she had to say, "Holy shit! Did you see that thing Michel made????? Did you get that????" I thought she was talking about Josiah's brother Michael; How did I miss something he made? Then a picture came through of artwork with Josiah on it.

"Where did you see this?" I wrote frantically.

"Instagram!"

"What is this masterpiece!!! I want one. How did we not know about this!?"

"I am so confused." she wrote.

I immediately went to Instagram and found the picture and wrote the artist, telling her I was Josiah's mom. In the meantime, Rain tells me she is private messaging her, then writes, "Wait she is writing me... I am calling her; I will call you."

I wait. Baffled!

Rain called to tell me of their conversation, and then I called her also. This beautiful artist's name is Michela. Her older sister, Kirsten, was one of Josiah's roommates in Santa Cruz. Kirsten had told Michela that she should come out and meet Josiah. That they had so much in common, that they thought alike and did similar art. Michela had planned on a visit, but Josiah left before they could meet. She said she had felt a connection with him even though they never met. She was creating art for her portfolio to present to different art schools she was applying for, and got a vision of doing art with Josiah in mind. As she began to create it, she felt him guiding her. She said she felt like she was creating it for his family, and especially for me! She had finished her art project and posted it on the 22nd not even aware that it was the day he ascended. I sat there with the phone at my ear and my mind blown.

"Who does this?" I cried, as that tidal wave finally had a place to crescendo. How is this possible? Josiah had done something beyond my capability of understanding, yet it was true. Josiah had channeled art, through an imaginative stranger. A painting of himself, with his wooden wonders engraved on it, from the ethers! Josiah had given me Art on Oct 22nd, 2019. Two years from the day he left this planet. I was dumb-founded.

That night I went to meditation to hopefully collect all this and put it in one place inside me. My friend Michelle, the same one I had gone to Sedona with and experienced all the number sequences, had met me there and when it was over, we sat in my car exchanging stories. I was blowing her away with all that had happened, and as I was telling her about the eighty-eights and pointing to my odometer, it was at 088226! Seriously, 88 and 22? "Thank you, Josiah!" I shouted.

And, somewhere in the midst of all this, I had connected that the tattoos behind my ears, those vibrations of love and light and truth and wisdom; were Reiki. I had Reiki my ears, permanently!

Halloween 2019

Halloween has always been a favorite holiday for me. Aside from all the gruesome storylines, I have always enjoyed dressing up. My infamous gypsy attire, which most people say is my everyday wardrobe, with added jewels and extra thick makeup. Last year, I was able to join in with the kids, dress up and wander the streets, watching the kids jacked up on sugar and begging for more. The one day of the year you *can* take candy from a stranger. But this year I was still in a funk. Even after all the mind-blowing gifts Josiah had presented, I was still just so-so. I sat over at Jeremy's and Aimee's, telling them I was going to go home instead of street walking with them.

"Are you sure?" Aimee questioned. This girl is ridiculously in tune with me, and she was hoping I would take pause, before I regretted not joining in. She was right to ask.

"If my cozy wrap is in the car I will go!" I told them, like the wrap would be my sign, or my out. My evening would be decided by the warmth of my mother's wrap that was maybe in the car. Gratefully, it was. This year there would be no gypsy costume. However, I was about to don myself with a lost part of me I was not aware had survived and was about to reappear.

This year Aimee's costume was a head-to-toe full body alien. Far from truly scary, yet unnervingly eerie and funny. Her costume set the tone for the evening, and the joking that emerged, for this girl's ability to pull off this body suit of a costume. We roamed the streets. Houses lit up, side by side one another with firepits, wailing music and cauldrons of candy. Some of the tightly woven homes had little room for the kids to squeeze by, without banging into the homeowner's cars. I witnessed it over and over. I made a few silly quips here and there, and then went on to question, "Don't they know about Halloween Feng Shui?"

Aimee's friend was with us, and turned to me and said, "You are so funny!" Now, *this* comment had caused a pause in me. I am funny, I thought! I had not heard anyone say that to me in a long while. We continued our Halloween evening. She had no idea the impact her comment had had on me!

As I was driving home, I took that comment off the shelf of my mind. I realized I had been able to laugh and joke. I was interacting like a younger version of myself. Before cancer had showed itself in the body of my child and ravished its way through all of us. I thought of my kids, my husband and everyone that had journeyed with me these years. How much of me they have missed. I had not abandoned them. I had abandoned myself. Tears blurred my vision as the streetlight made its way from red to green. The intersection crossing was like a threshold from one realization to the next.

And then I heard him. *"Mom! I told you to Reiki your ears, not only so you could hear me, I had you Reiki your ears so you could also hear yourself again."*

November 1: Butterfly Dream

I woke up at five a.m. knowing I had been dreaming intensely. I wiggled myself out of bed, dazed, stumbling to turn on the coffee pot, searching for recollection, but I was too tired this morning. I needed more sleep. An hour later, I woke with that same knowing, but no memory of what had appeared. I knew it was about Josiah, but I could not find him. I stumbled to the coffeemaker and sat as the morning clouds receded in the sky. Coffee mixed with the still of morning, I closed my eyes to take inventory. And then one amazing memory appeared. I remembered my dream!

I saw myself lying down outside, looking up to the sky. Above me was a butterfly hovering. Josiah's energy. In my dream, I took out my phone to take his picture, but I could not, because the butterfly was flying towards me.

273

It landed on my lips. I held my phone out to take this momentous picture and noticed the wings were moving. I began to video what was happening! Telepathically conversing with Josiah while sending the video to Jeremy, Valerie, and all my friends and family. The wings movement was slow and steady. Calm and comforting. I laid still. "My words are on your lips; you speak, and I speak with you!" he tells me. "Is this about the book? I questioned. "Am I done?"

"This is about forever!" he said. I woke before the butterfly flew away, which told me it, and he, never will.

I felt guided to pull three cards from the deck Talking to Heaven. I laughed and cried as the first card fell on my lap. *I send you loving signs through nature.* The card's picture is a butterfly on a dandelion.

The second card: *I have become one of your guides.* The picture on it is a person reaching up towards heaven and an arm reaches down towards them. I love when this card flies out, confirming what has been told to me so often.

The third card always makes me quiver. *Although you may not understand it now, everything happens for a reason.* The picture on it is two hands holding out a puzzle piece that are about to interlock into each other.

Like the butterfly on my lips, he remains. Our puzzle pieces fitting perfectly together! Josiah is walking with me, guiding me. Sending me signs. My words are his words, and his are mine. Our journey continues and our bond is forever.

I asked him for one more message through these cards. It takes a minute for a card to appear. I exhaust

The Translucent Door

"Welcome back, Josiah," whorled the Ethereal. Josiah looked around, integrating his surroundings and stabilizing his magenta light body.

"Wow, that was a surprise, and intense! I wasn't expecting that!" he proclaimed.

"I thought I was just going to peek inside the opening. It seemed as if the forest had parted, like a curtain opening to an audience of trees and rivers and the most brilliant ocean I had ever seen. The forest creatures and Angels were singing. In that moment I knew there was no other way to travel."

"It was exclusively created for you. You were the only one that could see it. The Translucent Doorway to here."

"I thought I had more time. I was healing!"

"Remember, this time was a shorter visit. One that taught you to teach them, about us. It was time, you had done all you were supposed to do, Josiah," the Ethereal said as golden rays of memories filled the cosmos surrounding Josiah.

"I told everyone that weird dis-ease this world tried to put on me was not going to take me out!" Josiah replied matter-a-factly.

"You did, and you exceeded my expectations of what you could, and would, accomplish there."

"I did?" he responded unsurely and then he heard

the tears. "Ethereal, what is that? I hear crying?"

"That is the sound of every single person that knew you and loved you!"

"Why are they crying? They all knew I was on a path to healing! Look at me, I am fine. I am right here; I can hear them."

The Ethereal sighed. "Josiah, they are going to miss your physical presence, and not everyone understands this, or believes, that you can hear them!"

"Listen, Ethereal, one is so loud I can feel it inside my energetic body. What is happening? Who is that?"

"That is your mother, Josiah!"

"My mother, my mother. I have never had to leave her this way. I never wanted to make her cry. How can we do this to my mother? Make her stop!" He cried as he wiped translucent tears from his eyes and held them to the amethyst ray that illuminated his chest, just as he had done before he came to this lifetime.

"Make her stop!"

"I can't, Josiah, but you can!"

"I can? How?"

"In as many ways as you choose! You can stay with her, and with them. Use your Sacred Alchemy to manifest in any way you choose, to show her you are okay and communicate. Your bond with her continues from here!"

"MOM! MOM! I Love you!! Look with your heart! Look with your soul! Look with your Spirit!

MOM! Look! I am in everything!"

Closing Thoughts

June 2020

Now there is a baby coming. Valerie is expecting, and it is a boy. Is this Josiah reincarnated? My mom? My dad? Or is this a new soul that will teach us another lesson about the gift of this tapestry we call life?

I know she is secretly wanting to name him Josiah, but knows that might be too hard on me, on all of us. Secretly I wish she would too. Yet, that might lead me to thievery, making that child my own. I speak in jest, sort of. I have already claimed my grandchildren as my own, hardly ever referring to them as my grandchildren unless it is warranted.

This baby deserves his own individuality, with a splash of Oochawad! If it is Josiah, we will know in my next writing. Or, maybe I will write about my mother as she demanded! Maybe sibling grief? Maybe about Angels and Energy? Maybe about being a child of the 60's and 70's, hair bands, Sweet & Low, fat-free Frankenfood and delicious delusional dieting? Or maybe about my multiple marriages, and the wisdom I needed from them.

All of them have woven their colors through me. Dull, and vibrant threads, creating the eclectic fabric that is me. The frayed edges only add to its antique-ish charm.

At least I hope you see that.

Until then, I marvel at where I am. I marvel at how we as mothers, as humans, have the capacity to strengthen these threads, by extending them to each other's tapestries, creating the most interwoven majestic and divine scenery of love.

When I look at your tapestry, I do not see all the messes in the miles. I see the beauty in your history, (Her-story) Your story!

Your story is beautifully broken and a magnificent masterpiece, illuminated by the Spirit of your child.

My goodness, it is amazing!

I cannot even fathom that I just wrote that. Where the hell did that come from?

Well, we know now.

The Ethereal in me, sitting with Josiah, speaking to the Ethereal in you, sitting with your child.

Back in that schoolyard dream, Josiah asked me, *"Can I stay with you?"*

I could have shut down.

I could have called it quits.

I could have damned this world and the Ethereal—

But I didn't.

I said, "Yes!"

I chose to be polished,

Because of Josiah!

Beauty, Strength & Healing,

Raina Irene

Thank you

I could go on. There have been more signs, and there will be more after this book is done. My bond with Josiah will continue to grow, just as your bond to your child will. I feel so humbled and so fortunate that I had the nudge of his Spirit to keep my fingers on the keyboard. Typing to you the truth of my experiences has been a gift, you have given to me! The gift of freedom. The gift of expansion. The gift of honesty, and the gift of authenticity.

I thank you, Sacred Mommaz.

Thank You to Shanda Trofe. You are so much more than my publisher. You listened and coached me to be unapologetic in my journey. Knowing that writing this was my therapy. You held me when writing these stories was kicking my ass, and patiently allowed me to continue in my own time. I love you.

Thank you to the multiple authors that have become my friends, and my biggest cheerleaders.

Thank you to my Soul Sisters who have listened as I read you countless stories. You know who you are, and I am eternally grateful.

Thank you to my sister Sheri. You are my person.

Thank you to Rain for continuing to share your life, love, support and creative expression with me.

Thank you, Michael, for the hours you spend talking with me about your brother.

Thank you, Brian, for being my confidant!

Thank you to My Beauty, Valerie, for holding me together and putting my puzzle pieces back in their proper position.

Thank you, Jeremy, My Strength, for being just that, My strength. For helping me divide and conquer, and for always answering your phone!

Thank you to Aimee, my right arm, my soul daughter. You know what my heart needs, and you make sure it has it. I am so grateful!

Thank you to Valerie H, my other soul daughter, for your open heart and listening spirit.

Thank you to my grandchildren. You are the liquid gold that fills my heart, filling in the broken lines!

Thank you to the Riches of my life, my husband, my tree trunk. When my earth shifted, you made sure I did not fall too far.

Thank you, Mitchell, without you, there would not have been them!

Thank you, Josiah,

My healing son,

For choosing me!

Life is so precious, you can't go it alone,

We're all so connected, and we'll rise as one!

I say hey Josiah, thank you Josiah

In our hearts we hold you so dear

Because of Josiah

About the Author

*R*aina Irene is a *Heart, Soul, Spirit Practitioner* and the owner of *Beauty, Strength & Healing Inc.*

She is a Licensed Esthetician and holds multiple certificates in Holistic Health, Spiritual and Emotional Healing, Plant Medicine, Reiki, Angels and the Afterlife. Raina's eclectic and spiritual diversity enables her to tap into your unique needs, supporting and guiding you to clarity and connecting you with your own healing energies.

Raina holds Healing Circles with the emphasis on Inner Wisdom and Understanding Grief. Educating from a heart of experience.

From an early age, Raina was aware of the Spirit world. When she was a teenager her older sister went to Spirit, greatly impacting her view on life, and what was afterward. In her early thirties, after her father's transition, she began an even deeper exploration into the afterlife; however, it was her son's sudden departure in 2017, that shifted her awareness, and took her on a journey from heart-shattering grief, to the realization that their bond is unbreakable, living and still possible.

With her son-in-Spirit serving as her teacher, she learned to recognize, interpret and respond to the messages we receive from the ones we love in Spirit.

She now works with mothers who have children-in-Spirit, helping them to understand that communication with their child is not only possible, but happening all the time.

All you have to do is Believe, and you *will* see. Love is forever...

Our bonds Continue...

Like Raina's page:

www.facebook.com/gypsyraina

Join Raina's group:
www.facebook.com/groups/BeautyStrengthHealing

And for the Mother's with a child in Spirit

Join her group
www.facebook.com/groups/lullabyletters

For resource links and pictures, and to set up a chat with Raina, or to acquire about her Oracle Deck, created with Josiah's art and Sacred messages...

Sacred Alchemy:
Connecting you to the ones you love in Spirit

www.rainairene.love

"I am an awakened being. I am one with the stars and one with the earth. I am one with the Universe. Inspiration pulses from within my heart. I see, feel and move in creation as it always has been. A start, never an end. The fractal doorway opens magically to the wisdom within, as it leads me down the rabbit hole that splits infinity forever. Soaring into the expansive morning of a sunrise, I see the rainbow cast across the horizon just as that moment capsizes. Gazing one star to another as the light pierces deep into the darkness which becomes ever so bright. The lie becomes illuminated, tis seen and from once it came, it again can now be free. Veils thinning, light growing, love bursting from within. The lies spiral out, clarity moves in. Space is created for time that is eternal. Truth is only left, is the only thing to be seen. Weightless, **we** dance into that sunrise for another round has begun to show its true colors. Colors that have never before been seen. Whispers in the wind blow by as the conscious mind blinks an eye. Awakened, the love surrounding you beams, as this new creation comes through."

~Josiah "Akoya" David

Josiah "Akoya" David

BELOVED

Made in the USA
Las Vegas, NV
21 August 2023

76400897R00177